Agora Excavations, 1931–2006

A Pictorial History

Craig A. Mauzy

with contributions by John McK. Camp II

The American School of Classical Studies at Athens

*To Marie, my wife, and Carl, my son, who have seen
only a shadow of me these past months*

*and to all the photographers who have captured and preserved
a visual record of our work during the past 75 years*

Photographer's shadow cast near the north entrance to the Agora, April 2006

CONTENTS

Preface

The year 2006 marks the 75th anniversary of the inauguration of systematic excavations by the American School of Classical Studies at Athens, itself celebrating its 125th anniversary this year, on the site of the ancient Athenian Agora. This seems a good time to summarize briefly the history and accomplishments of a project—still in progress—that has drawn upon the talents and resources of hundreds of individuals who have worked together to enhance our understanding of ancient Athens and its development through the ages.

This book does not pretend to be a systematic account of the excavations. It is rather a series of vignettes, celebrating key events and notable people in the project's history. The stories told are illustrated with many contemporary materials and photographs, and the text draws extensively on primary sources—notebooks, letters, and official documents. Generations of staff photographers, including Hermann Wagner, Alison Frantz, Jim Heyle, Eugene Vanderpool Jr., Robert Vincent Jr., and Craig A. Mauzy, have contributed to this volume.

After a short description of the ancient Athenian Agora, there is an account of the first season of excavations, starting in May 1931, when workmen with horses and carts began clearing the tons of spoil that overlay the area. The recording systems set up then have remained largely unchanged, and some of the first notebooks, photographs, and catalogue cards are displayed.

Three ambitious initiatives of 50 years ago are then presented: the reconstruction of the 2nd-century B.C. Stoa of Attalos as a museum and storage space for the vast amount of archaeological material found on the site; the restoration of the Byzantine Church of the Holy Apostles; and the landscaping of the archaeological park. The experience of any visitor to the modern site is still shaped by these major projects, which also reflect the generosity of the foundations and individuals who continue to make the work of the Agora Excavations possible.

The book finishes with a tribute to the staff and student volunteers who have contributed to this massive undertaking. Hundreds of publications contain the fruit of their labors, and a list of those published by the American School is provided.

Recovering the traces of social, political, and cultural life in the world's most ancient democracy continues to be an intellectual adventure story worth documenting. It is in this celebratory spirit that the book is presented.

THE AGORA AND THE EXCAVATIONS

1. View of the west side of the Agora at the start of excavations in Section A, June 19, 1931. View from the north toward the hill of Kolonos Agoraios and the Hephaisteion.

2. View looking southeast across the area of the ancient Agora on the day excavations began, May 25, 1931

THE AGORA 75 YEARS AGO

Excavations in the Athenian Agora by the American School of Classical Studies at Athens commenced in 1931 under the supervision of T. Leslie Shear. An area designated Section E was the first to be excavated. It was located in front of the Church of Panagia Vlassarou and just east of the wall enclosing Section OE (Old Excavation), an area explored by the German Archaeological Institute in the late 1890s.

3 & 4. *"After proper ceremony of sprinkling of holy water by priest of neighboring church* [Panagia Vlassarou] *Agora Excavations began about 7:30 a.m. Digging confined to area occupied by House 22 until it shall be levelled off. 28 men / 135 wagons"* (Notebook [Nb.] E I, p. 74; May 25, 1931).

5. View of the ancient Agora after 75 years of excavations, taken from a similar vantage point as **2**

THE AGORA IN ANTIQUITY

The Agora of Athens was the center of the ancient city: a large, open square where the citizens could assemble for a wide variety of purposes. On any given day the space might be used as a market, or for an election, a dramatic performance, a religious procession, military drill, or athletic competition. Here administrative, political, judicial, commercial, social, cultural, and religious activities all found a place together in the heart of Athens, and the square was surrounded by the public buildings necessary to run the Athenian government. These buildings, along with monuments and small objects, illustrate the important role it played in all aspects of public life. The council chamber, magistrates' offices, mint, and archives have all been uncovered, while the lawcourts are represented by the recovery of bronze ballots and a water-clock used to time speeches. The use of the area as a marketplace is indicated by the numerous shops where potters, cobblers, bronzeworkers, and sculptors made and sold their wares.

6. Model of the Agora in ca. 400 B.C., from the southeast

7. Lower colonnade of the Stoa of Attalos

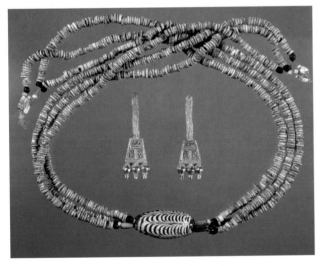

8. Early Geometric jewelry found in a burial

9. Ostrakon cast against Themistokles, 5th century B.C.

Long stoas (colonnades) (7) provided shaded walkways for those wishing to meet friends to discuss business, politics, or philosophy, while statues and commemorative inscriptions reminded citizens of former triumphs. A library and concert hall met cultural needs, and numerous small shrines and temples received regular worship. Given the prominence of Athens throughout much of antiquity, the Agora provides one of the richest sources for our understanding of the Greek world in antiquity.

Used as a burial ground (8) and for scattered habitation in the Bronze and Iron Ages, the area was first laid out as a public space in the 6th century B.C. Administrative buildings and small sanctuaries were built, and water was made available at a fountainhouse fed by an early aqueduct. Following the total destruction of Athens at the hands of the Persians in 480 B.C., the city was rebuilt and public buildings were added to the Agora one by one throughout the 5th and 4th centuries, when Athens contended for the hegemony of Greece. It is during this "Classical" period that the Agora and its buildings were frequented by statesmen such as Themistokles (9), Perikles, and Demosthenes, by the poets Aeschylos, Sophokles, Euripides, and Aristophanes, by the writers Thucydides and Herodotos, by artists such as Pheidias and Polygnotos, and by philosophers such as Sokrates, Plato, and Aristotle. Together, they were responsible for creating a society and culture that has set a standard against which subsequent human achievements have been judged. The Agora was the focal point of their varied activities and here the concept of democracy was first developed and practiced.

With the rise of Macedon under Philip II and Alexander the Great and during the subsequent Hellenistic period, all significant military, economic, and political power shifted to the East. In the spheres of education and philosophy, however, Athens maintained her preeminence. The Academy, founded by Plato, and the Lyceum, founded by Aristotle, continued to flourish. They were supplemented by the arrival of Zeno of Kition, who chose to lecture at the Agora in the Painted Stoa. Athenian cultural dominance continued throughout the Roman period, and the buildings added to the Agora reflect the educational role of the city, a role that ended only with the closing of the pagan philosophical schools by the Christian emperor Justinian in A.D. 529. With the collapse of security in the empire, Athens and the Agora suffered from periodic invasions and destructions: the Herulians in the 3rd century, the Visigoths in the 4th, the Vandals in the 5th, and the Slavs in the 6th. Following the Slavic invasion the area of the Agora was largely abandoned and neglected for close to 300 years.

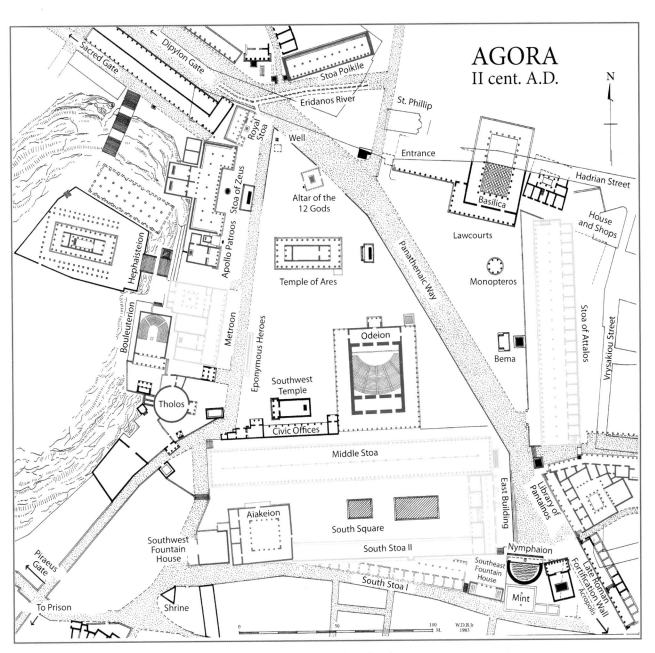

AGORA
II cent. A.D.

N

Sacred Gate
Dipylon Gate
Stoa Poikile
Eridanos River
St. Phillip
Royal Stoa
Well
Entrance
Hadrian Street
Basilica
Apollo Patroos
Stoa of Zeus
Altar of the 12 Gods
Lawcourts
House and Shops
Hephaisteion
Temple of Ares
Monopteros
Metroon
Bouleuterion
Eponymous Heroes
Odeion
Bema
Stoa of Attalos
Vrysakiou Street
Southwest Temple
Tholos
Southwest Temple
Civic Offices
Middle Stoa
East Building
Library of Pantainos
Aiakeion
South Square
South Stoa II
Piraeus Gate
Southwest Fountain House
Southeast Fountain House
Nymphaion
South Stoa I
Mint
Late Roman Fortification Wall
Acropolis
To Prison
Shrine

0   50   100
M.

W.D.B.Jr
1983

10. Plan of the Agora at the height of its development in ca. A.D. 150

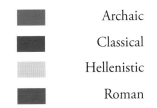

Archaic

Classical

Hellenistic

Roman

11. Aerial view of the Agora Excavations taken by the Greek Topographical Service, July 5th, 1933

THE SITE

The Agora lies on sloping ground northwest of the Acropolis, below and east of the extraordinarily well-preserved Doric temple of Hephaistos, popularly known as the "Theseion" (**11:a**). The marble giants (**11:b, 12**), reused as the facade of a Late Roman complex, were always visible, as was the north end of the Stoa of Attalos, preserved to its full height. The other ancient remains were not so well preserved, however, and their ruins lay as much as 8 meters below the modern surface, covered from the 10th century by an extensive neighborhood of private houses. The houses were repeatedly rebuilt, after successive invasions by Franks, Ottomans, and Venetians. The last destruction occurred in 1826, the result of a siege of the Acropolis during the Greek War of Independence. Once again the neighborhood was totally rebuilt, and only limited archaeological excavation was possible. The Stoa of Attalos (**11:c**) was cleared of debris by the Greek Archaeological Society in 1859/1862 and 1898/1902, the extension of the Athens/Piraeus railroad (**11:d**) cut through the northern part of the site in 1890/1, and other areas (e.g., **11:e**) were opened up by German and Greek archaeologists in 1896/7 and 1907/8. Except for these scattered and limited attempts, the remains of the center of ancient Athens lay deeply buried, inaccessible, and largely forgotten.

The challenges of excavation were considerable. The site has been occupied almost continuously for close to 5,000 years, so the stratigraphy is disturbed and complex. In addition, as well as sharing all the logistical problems inherent in any large-scale urban excavation, the Agora site must be one of the few where a street and a railway divide the area of the excavations (current excavations, **11:f**)

12. The so-called Stoa of the Giants and Tritons before the start of demolition in the central area of the Agora. View looking south, 1935.

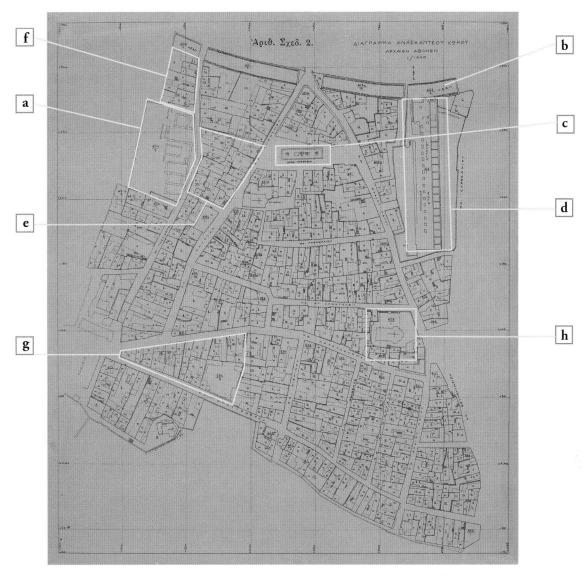

13. A drawing of the house lots in the area to be excavated: (**a**) Section OE, excavated by the German Archaeological Institute; (**b**) Athens/Piraeus railroad; (**c**) Giants and Tritons; (**d**) Section ΣA, Stoa of Attalos; (**e**) Section E, demolition of houses begun April 20, 1931, excavations begun May 25, 1931; (**f**) Section A, demolition of houses begun May 28, 1931; (**g**) Section ΣT, demolition of houses begun August 17, 1931; (**h**) Church of the Holy Apostles.

The Excavations

The systematic excavation of this important site was entrusted by the Greek State to the American School of Classical Studies, founded in Athens in 1881. Negotiations began in 1925, soon after the Greek parliament voted not to undertake the project itself, largely because of the huge costs of expropriation. The area in question covered some 24 acres and was occupied by 365 modern houses, all of which had to be purchased and demolished. Edward Capps, chairman of the Managing Committee of the American School, was the guiding spirit behind the project, and T. L. Shear was appointed the first field director. Shear assembled a staff that includes some of the best-known names in Greek archaeology: Homer A. Thompson, Eugene Vanderpool, Benjamin Meritt, Dorothy Burr (Thompson), Virginia Grace, Lucy Talcott, Alison Frantz, Piet de Jong, and John Travlos, among others. Actual work of excavation began in May of 1931, funded largely by John D. Rockefeller. Since then, several dozen more houses have been cleared, bringing the total to more than 400. The enterprise has been a huge one, both in terms of money and time. As is often the case with American cultural projects, the funding has been provided almost exclusively from private foundations and individuals: the Rockefeller Foundation, the Ford Foundation, the Mellon Foundation, the Kress Foundation, and the National Endowment for the Humanities have all participated. In recent years the work has been sustained by the David and Lucile Packard Foundation and the Packard Humanities Institute. Since 1931 hundreds of scholars, workers, specialists, and students have participated in the excavation, conservation, research, and publication of the site and its related finds. Collectively, they are responsible for one of the most productive archaeological projects in the Mediterranean basin. Over forty volumes and hundreds of scholarly articles have been published, adding much to our understanding of all aspects of ancient Greek history and society.

The Notebooks

The process of excavating an archaeological site is essentially destructive but the irrevocable features are preserved in a notebook. The excavator records his or her thoughts and observations, and uses drawings and photographs to supplement the text. After an excavation has concluded, scholars rely on the notebook to study the excavation, and it is through the notebooks that we may reconstruct the initial days of work in the Athenian Agora.

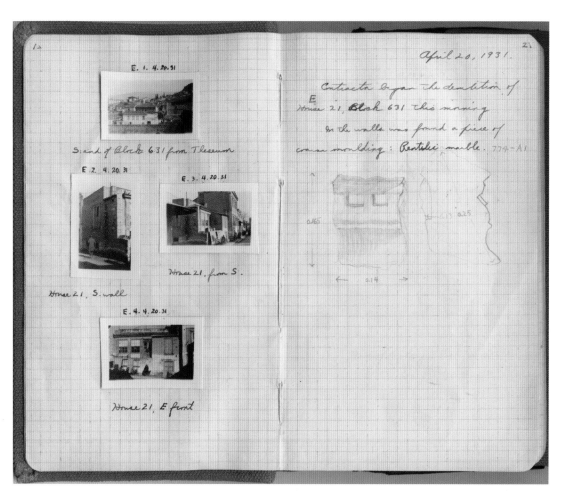

14. The first two pages of Nb. E I, dated April 20, 1931. Pasted on the first page are contact prints of images of the first building to be demolished before excavation of the area could begin. An entry notes, *"Contractor began the demolition of House 21, Block 631 (Section E) this morning. In the walls was found a piece of coarse moulding: Pentelic marble."*

15. The first building to be demolished, House 21, Block 631 (Section E). View looking north along Patousa Street.

16. Recent record shot of A 1, the first architectural find to be catalogued

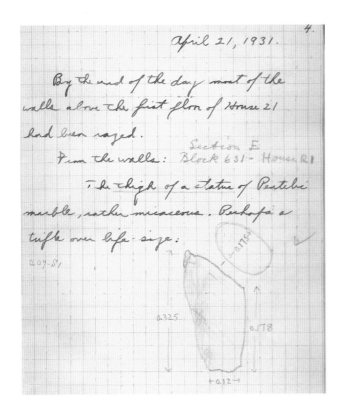

17. *"By the end of the day most of the walls above the first floor of House 21 had been razed. From the walls: the thigh of a statue of Pentelic marble, rather micaceous. Perhaps a trifle over life-size"* (Nb. E I, p. 4; April 21, 1931).

Fragments of many sculptures and architectural pieces were found in the walls of the buildings that were being demolished. The first catalogued pieces of the Architecture and Sculpture series were retrieved during the demolition of House 21. This is not surprising as the modern city was built on top of the ancient and the antiquities were easily available sources of building materials.

18. House 21 at the end of the first day of demolition

19. A view looking east from the Hephaisteion on April 27, 1931. The accompanying notebook entry reads, *"The walls of the upper storey of House 20 fall a prey to the minions of the εργολάβος [contractor]"* (Nb. E 1, p. 18).

Photography

A photograph made using the traditional silver halide process is a visual record largely unaltered by the photographer. It is this quality of capturing a mirrored image of the scene that lends itself to archaeological photography. Photography has been an essential component of the documentary process from the beginning of excavations at the Agora. The photograph, whether taken by the excavator or by the staff photographer, is an irreplaceable visual record of the excavation's progress. Stored in the project's photographic archive are over 300,000 images documenting the excavations and catalogued objects.

20 *(above)* & **21** *(right)*. From the beginning of excavations, the photographic record can be divided into the use of large-format and small-format cameras. Hermann Wagner, a member of the German Archaeological Institute, was the first staff photographer. He was primarily responsible for the large-format photography, using a view camera that required 18 × 24 cm glass negatives. These large-format images, even to this day, are unequalled for the amount of information that can be transmitted in a single image. On the right (**21**) is a detail enlarged from the 18 × 24 cm negative of the image above (**20**). The image was taken on the afternoon of May 25, 1931, and illustrates the work accomplished during the first day of excavations in Section E. The buildings on the west side of the Agora had been demolished in preparation for excavation, resulting in an unobstructed view from the Church of Panagia Vlassarou toward the Hephaisteion.

22:a–c. During this first season, Wagner returned to the same vantage point and took a series of images illustrating the progress of the work through time. In this way a step-by-step visual record was made of the excavations.

a. Early June 1931

b. June 19, 1931

c. July 22, 1931

15

23. The notebook entries are records of the excavator's observations and are not meant to be conclusive. Further excavation invariably reveals more information. On May 27, 1931, the excavator of Section E, Frederick O. Waagé, recorded this: *"A sudden very heavy thunderstorm at 3 p.m. deluges dig and completely fills excavations. Some of water drained off down well or cistern just N. of N. wall of E. room; after two hours, well or cistern in W. room opens and rest of water drains off there. No work, of course, for rest of day. Rope thrown around dig"* (Nb. E I, p. 94).

24 *(below)*. Nb. E I, pp. 93–94; May 27, 1931.

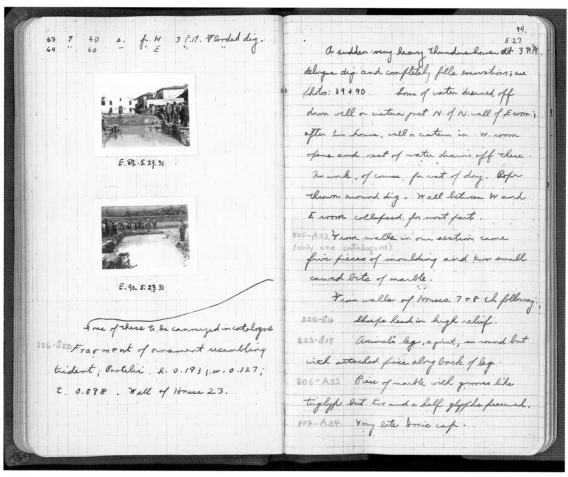

25. Later excavations reveal the Great Drain. T. Leslie Shear made these comments in his end-of-season excavation report:
"But while the problem of the disposal of the water was under consideration by the staff an underground vent was opened by the pressure of the water above it and the water flowed away with great celerity. The explanation of this fortunate occurrence was revealed at a later stage of the campaign by the discovery of a great drain or water-channel, which passes through this area in a direction from south to north and with a gentle slope towards the north" ("The Progress of the First Campaign of Excavation in 1931," *Hesperia* 2 [1933], p. 103).

26. View looking southeast across Section E on July 7, 1931, at 5 p.m.

Whereas the staff photographer was called upon to photograph the most important features with a large-view camera, the excavators were given a 35mm camera (a Leica) to record the day-to-day details of the progress of the excavations. This handheld camera was easy to carry about and use more spontaneously, and thus the Leica images reveal a more candid view of the work on the excavation. The photographs on this page are most likely those of Frederick O. Waagé, the excavator of Section E in 1931, and they show the range of images to be found in his notebooks. The photograph above (**26**) was taken from Poseidon Street (the west side of the Agora) looking southeast across Section E. In the foreground is the newest area of the section to be opened up; the Church of Panagia Vlassarou is visible in the middle, the Acropolis behind. Waagé labeled the photograph as an *"extracurricular photo of Acropolis."* The content of the image combines both archaeological and contemporary historical details. The images below (**27** & **28**) were taken to illustrate archaeological features. At bottom left is a photograph of a *"Marble Forearm found at bottom of S. part of drain."* At bottom right, the photograph shows a large storage jar or pithos, a seemingly mundane feature nevertheless documented, as it is the responsibility of the excavator to record all that is revealed in the course of excavation. Later scholarship will ascertain its archaeological importance.

27 (left) & *28 (below)*

29. Sometimes the photographer himself has been captured on film. T. Leslie Shear, director of the excavations and an accomplished photographer, was caught recording the discovery of a herm (S 33).

"In 5/A at -2.50 was found a herm lying on its side; it had formed the support of a large statue of a draped woman? holding a child on the left arm which rested on the top of the Herme, child's body preserved up to just above waist. Total height preserved: 1.36 m" (Nb. E I, p. 140; June 4, 1931).

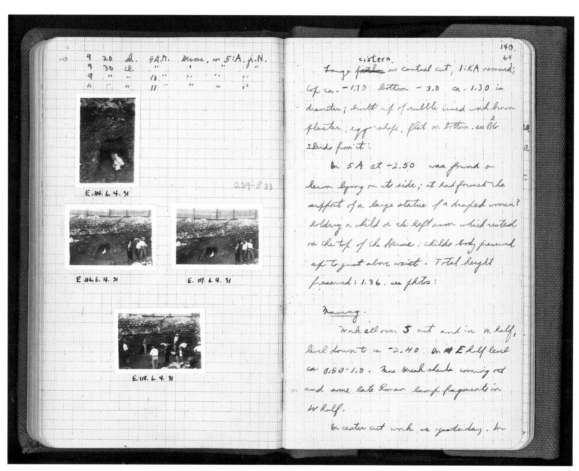

30 *(above)*. Nb. E I, pp. 139–140; June 4, 1931.

31:a, b. The herm as photographed by T. Leslie Shear, June 4, 1931, 11 a.m.

THE CARD CATALOGUE

A card catalogue system has been used since the beginning of the excavations to record the important information related to inventoried objects. Lucy Talcott, one of the original members of the Agora Excavations staff, is credited with its development into an elaborately cross-referenced record system. The catalogue card became the most important link to all the relevant data concerning an object and has only recently been replaced by a digital database.

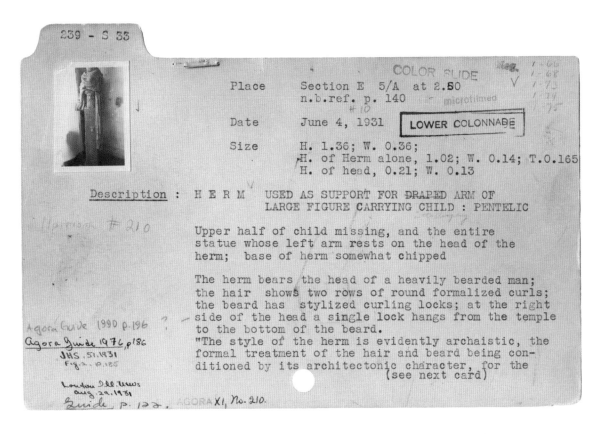

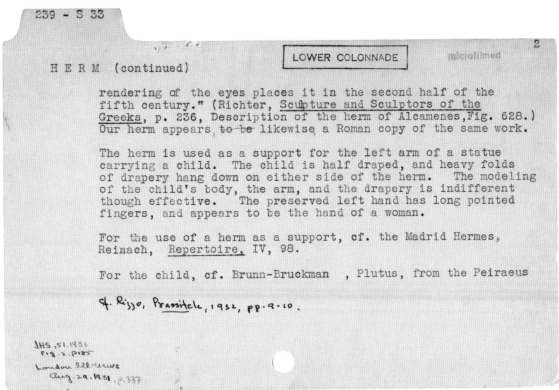

32. Catalogue card of the herm S 33, discovered June 4, 1931, in Section E

THE ALTAR OF ZEUS REDISCOVERED

The Agora Excavations began with the aim of revealing the monuments and history of the ancient Agora. Of course, every artifact or feature that was exposed held importance, but when something extraordinary was brought to light, its discovery generated great excitement. On July 23, 1931, the excavator filled five pages of his notebook describing a significant discovery of the first excavation season: *"A large structure once covered a large part of* [the] *area, it was almost certainly an Altar."* A few pages later he added another entry describing an *"Altar Block: the large block of white marble with moulding above and below; shown on photos p. 507"* (Nb. E III, pp. 503–507). The altar was later identified as the Altar of Zeus Agoraios, an important ancient monument believed to have been erected first on the Pnyx in the 4th century B.C. and later dismantled and reerected at the turn of the millenium in its present location.

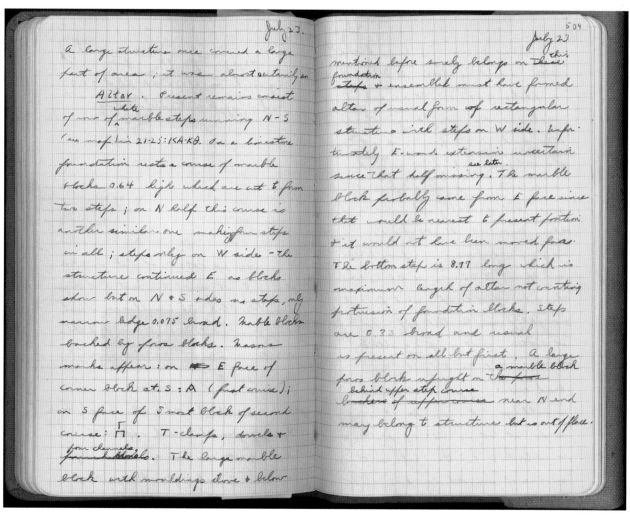

33. Nb. E III, pp. 503–504; July 23, 1931.

34. T. Leslie Shear, director of the excavations, inspecting the newly discovered altar, 1931

35. View of the orthostate block (A 404) of the Altar of Zeus Agoraios

36. View looking northeast across Section E at the end of the 1931 season. Visible in the foreground is a column base and foundation blocks of the Metroon; to the left, the statue of Emperor Hadrian was found lying in the Great Drain. In the center background are the steps of the Altar of Zeus Agoraios and its large altar block. Visible in the middle foreground are the foundations for the monument of the Eponymous Heroes. The Church of Panagia Vlassarou is visible in the upper right corner.

THERE NEVER IS ENOUGH TIME

Inevitably something is found at the end of the excavation season that must be left for the next season to fully explore. Just a few days after the discovery of the Altar of Zeus Agoraios, exploration of the Great Drain was progressing on the west side of Section E when the excavator noted another surprising find: *"Digging away earth between cover slab and this block was found Statue of Roman Emperor, preserved from just below kilt to about shoulders, lying at a slant, lower part resting on low end of the fallen cover slab and body slanting down and outward to E."* The difficulty of making a fuller description and taking photographs is apparent in a later comment, *"Earth roof must be supported and large block broken and removed before statue can be taken out"* (Nb. E III, p. 518). The statue would remain lying in the ground until it could be properly excavated and removed at the beginning of the following season.

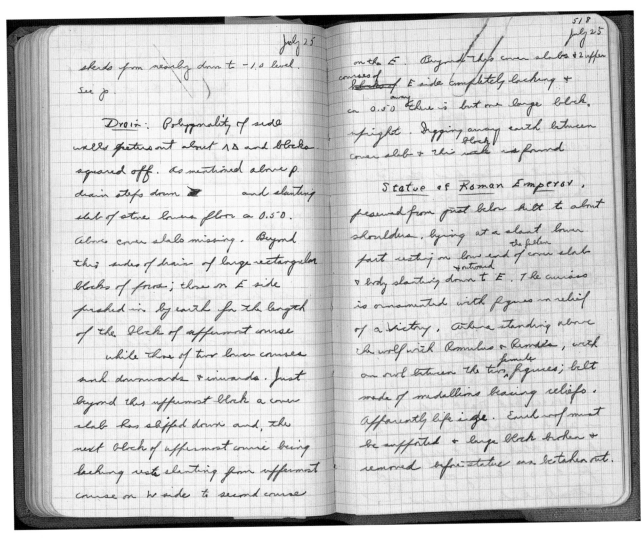

37. Nb. E III, pp. 517–518; July 25, 1931.

38. The statue, identified as a portrait of the emperor Hadrian (S 166), was covered with wood to protect it until it could be lifted the following season.

39. The statue of Hadrian lying face down in the Great Drain, February 5, 1932

40. Lifting the statue to an upright position

41. Cleaning and preparing to photograph the statue

42. The first formal photographic portrait of the statue of Hadrian

43. T. Leslie Shear, director of the excavations, and Edward Capps, chairman of the Managing Committee, pose with the statue of Hadrian, 1932.

The Workmen of the Excavations

During the first week of excavations, 29 workmen were employed at a daily salary of 60 drachmas per day (46). The normal workweek was Monday to Saturday so a workman's salary was 360 drachmas per week. By June of 1931 over 100 workmen were employed. During the early seasons, removing the immense amount of accumulated fill was accomplished without the use of machinery. The buildings were torn down as they had been built, largely by hand. After the buildings were demolished and the debris removed, the actual excavations began. The excavator of Section E kept a daily record of the men working in his area and the number of horse carts filled each day. May 29th would be the busiest day of the 1931 season (44). He recorded in his notebook that 26¾ men worked in his area and that 231 carts were filled (45). And where did all of this material go? *The carting away of the excavated material was done by contract, let after competition to the lowest bidder, and the contractor secured from the police the designation of places for dumping, which were outside of the city, along the sacred way to Eleusis* (*Hesperia* 2 [1933], p. 101). As the season progressed antiquities were discovered which also had to be removed, and they were lifted by the workmen using the same tools and techniques as their predecessors: ropes, pallets, and group effort (47).

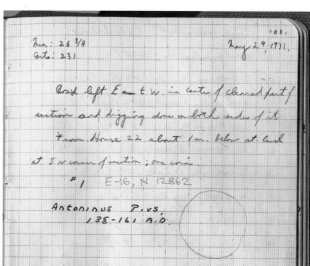

44. Horse cart "gridlock" in Section E, May 29, 1931   45. Detail of Nb. E I, p. 100; May 29, 1931.

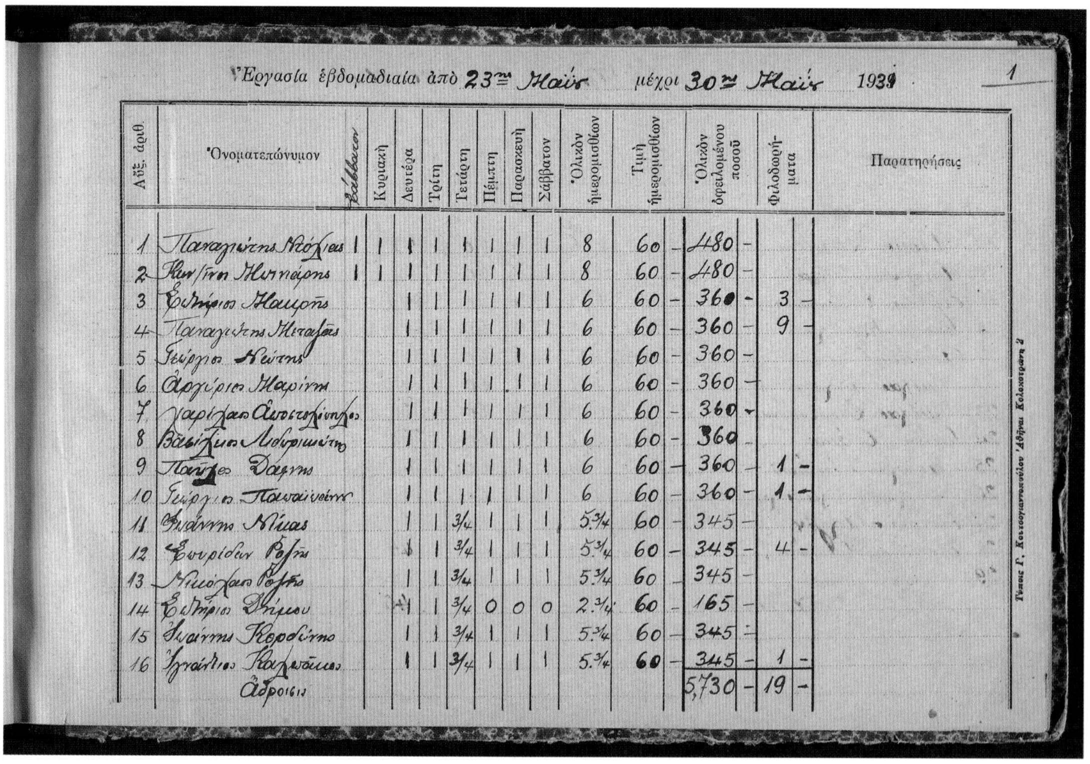

Αὔξ. ἀριθ	Ὀνοματεπώνυμον	Κυριακή	Δευτέρα	Τρίτη	Τετάρτη	Πέμπτη	Παρασκευή	Σάββατον	Ὁλικὸν ἡμερομισθίον	Τιμὴ ἡμερομισθίου	Ὁλικὸν ὀφειλομένου ποσοῦ	Φιλοδωρή-ματα	Παρατηρήσεις
1	Παναγιώτης Σκόρδας								8	60	480	–	
2									8	60	480	–	
3									6	60	360	3	
4									6	60	360	9	
5									6	60	360	–	
6									6	60	360		
7									6	60	360		
8									6	60	360		
9									6	60	360	1	
10									6	60	360	1	
11			¾						5¾	60	345		
12			¾						5¾	60	345	4	
13			¾						5¾	60	345		
14			¾	0	0	0			2¾	60	165		
15			¾						5¾	60	345		
16			¾						5¾	60	345	1	
	Ἄθροισμα										5,730	19	

46. The first page of the workmen's salary ledger

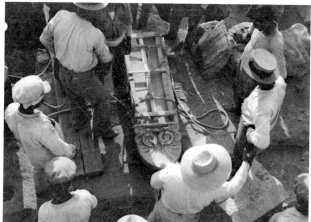

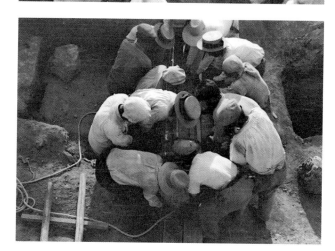

47:a–d *(above)*. Workmen moving a stele (I 69)

48:a–c *(above)*. Workmen and horse cart removing excavated fill from Section E

25

The Old Excavation House

The photograph below, taken in June of 1939, illustrates the extent of the Agora Excavations during the first eight years. The so-called Old Excavation House, located at Asteroskopeiou Street 25, was actually a group of houses that formed a complex of temporary storerooms and workspace for the early excavations (highlighted in yellow). All of the antiquities that had been found to date were stored in these buildings. Planning for the construction of a museum to properly display the important pieces and to house the enormous quantity of excavated material had already begun by 1939, but all work at the excavation was suspended in the spring of 1940 due to the start of World War II.

49. View from the Observatory looking east, showing the extent of excavations in June 1939. The Old Excavation House complex is highlighted in yellow.

50. Pottery storage adjoining the records office, where Lucy Talcott sits at her desk, 1937

51. The records office, 1937

52. Pottery mending room, 1937

53. Pot-menders at work, 1937

54. Alison Frantz in the photographic studio, 1937

55. John Travlos working in the architect's office, 1937

56. A view toward the southeast from the Hephaisteion in 1949. The houses in the middle foreground are the Old Excavation House complex. Note that this image, just over 50 years old, is from the first series of color transparencies of the Agora and introduces the use of color photography to the site.

Planning for a Museum

After the Second World War, *"work in the field was resumed in 1946 on a very small scale by special permit from the Greek Government to do supplementary work in areas already dug and to begin investigation of the site which had been selected for the museum by the joint decision of the Greek Government and the School. . . .*

In 1947 permission was given for larger-scale work on the museum site in the effort to complete the excavation and begin construction. Streets lined with private houses and shops and a trapezoidal enclosure . . . were found, and to clarify the approach to that area the southwest corner of the Agora was further cleared, revealing . . . chamber tombs and geometric graves.

By 1948 work on the museum site had shown that this residential-industrial area of the Classical period was too important to be covered and a new museum site must be found. Preliminary plans had already been drawn for a museum for which Rockefeller funds were specifically provided" (L. S. Meritt, *History of the American School of Classical Studies at Athens, 1939–1980* [1984], pp. 177–178).

57. A drawing of one of several alternative museum designs proposed to be built on the western side of the Agora in the valley between the Areopagus and the Pnyx. Design by the architectural firm W. S. Thompson & Phelps Barnum, 1947.

58. Sketch of another proposed museum design to be built on the western side of the Agora in the valley between the Areopagus and the Pnyx. The drawing illustrates the relationship of the site of the proposed museum to the Areopagus and the Acropolis in the background. Design by the architectural firm W. S. Thompson & Phelps Barnum, 1947.

59. View from the Observatory looking east, showing the proposed site of the original museum (highlighted in green). The site of the present-day Agora museum, in the reconstructed Stoa of Attalos, is highlighted in red. The Old Excavation House complex is highlighted in yellow. August 1947.

60. View from the excavation looking west, toward the hill of the Observatory. A temporary wooden frame has been erected to give an impression of a gable end of the proposed museum. August 1947.

61. The Stoa of Attalos in November of 1952

The Stoa of Attalos
Reconstruction

62. The Stoa of Attalos in December of 1956

CHANGE OF PLANS

In the following memorandum from 1948, Homer A. Thompson, then director of the Agora Excavations, presents the argument for seeking an alternative site for the Agora museum and proposes an ingenious solution: the reconstruction of the Stoa of Attalos. It would be five years before actual work began and another three years before the reconstruction of the stoa was complete. There were changes and alterations along the way, but the final result is remarkably true to what he and his staff originally envisioned.

Memorandum on a Project to Reconstruct the Stoa of Attalos to Serve as the Agora Museum

The Problem of the Site. The area to the west of the Areopagus which had been designated long ago as a site for the permanent Agora museum has now been almost completely explored. Although the site still retains most of the natural advantages that recommended its selection in the beginning, the excavations of the past season have brought to light so many ancient remains as to necessitate re-opening the whole question. These remains consist of a Mycenaean chamber tomb, an important stretch of ancient road, the foundations of a large enclosure of the fifth century B.C. apparently of a public nature, the foundations of houses and shops of both the Greek and Roman periods and a public bath. The construction of the museum according to the present plans would involve demolishing most of these remains and covering over practically all the rest.

The only alternative site that has been proposed hitherto is the Theseum Park. This site would have the disadvantage of being so remote from the Agora proper as to be thoroughly inconvenient for the further prosecution of the excavations and, still more serious, as to divorce the finds from their original setting. It would also require costly archaeological exploration which might well reveal antiquities that in their turn would have to be respected.

Within the Agora area proper there appears to be no place where a new building of sufficient size could be erected without either involving the destruction of important ancient remains or interfering in an intolerable way with the view of the ancient buildings and the neighboring hills.

To meet this impasse another solution has been proposed: the reconstruction of the Stoa of Attalos to house the museum.

Scheme and Present State of the Stoa. In plan the Stoa was a long rectangle measuring ca. 19.50 × 112 m. overall. Along its back was a row of 23 rooms measuring ca. 4.90 m. each square inside, all opening through single doors on a very broad porch with a row of 45 columns down the front and a row of 22 down its middle. All this was repeated in a second storey accessible by a stairway at each end. Along the whole front of the building ran a terrace some 6.5 m. wide, through most of its length rising well above the level of the square so as to command a superb view of the market place, the Areopagus, the Hill of the Nymphs and Kolonos Agoraios crowned by the Temple of Hephaistos.

The accompanying photographs [65, 66] will give an idea of the state of preservation of the building. At its northeast corner the walls still stand to their original height and one cornice block remains in position. The southeast corner is almost equally well preserved. The foundations for the back wall through most of the length of the building have been stripped to a little below floor level; the wall in front of the shops still retains its euthynteria and thresholds almost throughout and its orthostates in many places. The underpinning for the front steps and colonnade is intact over the northern 18 m. and southern 10 m.; elsewhere it has been pillaged to varying depths. Most of the piers for the interior columns have been dismantled to a great depth. Of the terrace wall only the lowest blocks remain in place. The marble superstructure of the building is now represented by a few dozen scattered blocks from columns, architrave, frieze, cornice, etc.

63. Aerial photograph of the Agora taken by the Greek Topographical Service on August 3, 1951. Area in green: the first site of the proposed Agora museum. Area in blue: a suggested alternative site for the museum in the Theseum Park. Area in red: the proposed site of the Agora museum in the reconstructed Stoa of Attalos. Area in yellow: the Old Excavation House complex.

64. Drawing of the proposed Stoa of Attalos reconstruction by G. P. Stevens, dated 1949

In general it may be said that enough remains to permit of the very complete and trustworthy restoration of the building, and that such a restoration could be effected without damaging or obscuring the ancient remains in a way to excite the criticism of the archaeologist. A certain amount of exploration has already been carried out beneath the Stoa, revealing the southeast corner of a large cloistered court that would seem to have been dismantled by the Stoa builders and also the foundations of some private houses. If further exploration of the same levels were deemed advisable in the future it could be effected by going down through the floors and would be little more costly than if carried out now.

Materials of the Stoa. The foundations consist of massive conglomerate blocks set into the bedrock. The walls are of gray Peiraeus limestone laid in courses alternately high and low, the high courses consisting of two blocks set on edge, the low courses of a single block running through the thickness of the wall. Steps, euthynteria and thresholds in the line of the shop fronts, the orthostates in the same wall and a string course above the orthostates, the jambs and lintels of the shop doors are of gray-blue Hymettian marble. White Pentelic marble was used for the front columns, architraves, friezes and cornice, and for the capitals and bases of the interior columns; the shafts of the interior columns appear to have been of limestone. The building was roofed with terracotta tiles.

In restoring the Stoa it would seem essential to use marble for the front parts, perhaps limestone for the walls, certainly terracotta tiles for the roof. The terrace wall along the front of the building might appropriately be rebuilt with scattered ancient blocks, great numbers of which now encumber the excavated area of the square.

Disposition of Space within the Building. Of the 23 original shops in the ground floor of the Stoa the cross walls are sufficiently preserved to necessitate the restoration of only the four southernmost; the remaining length of the walled part of the building on the ground floor and the whole length of the walled part on the upper floor might be divided at will. It would seem desirable, however, to respect the ancient divisions to the extent of restoring all 23 doorways at least on the ground floor, but glazing the openings to assist in the lighting of the back part. The double colonnade on the ground floor would certainly be kept unobstructed so as to give as far as possible the original effect. A longitudinal dividing wall, consisting for the most part of windows, might be carried the whole length of the building in the upper storey so as to leave a promenade of say 3 m. along the front and to increase enormously the enclosed space in the building. Additional space might be secured if necessary by running a narrow mezzanine floor along either side of the walled part of the building in the lower storey where the ceiling had a height of over 6 m.

The enclosed parts of the Stoa if restored as above would have a floor space of ca. 2,200 square meters, as compared with ca. 2,500 square meters in the present museum plans. There would be available in addition, however, the double colonnade on the ground floor with an area of ca. 1,400 square meters: ideal space for the display of heavy marbles architectural, sculptural and epigraphic. Inasmuch as the division of space within the main elements of the building would be elastic, it is clear that adequate space would be available for public exhibition galleries, for study groups and for storage. The provision for workrooms and offices such as will be necessary for the duration of the excavation might be made in such a way that this space could subsequently be utilized for storage or display.

If basement space were required for boiler room, plumbing, vaults, air-raid shelters, it could very readily be secured by removing the earth from within the massive foundations of any desired number of the shops in the northern part of the building where the foundations deepen to match the sloping ground level.

65. View of the north end of the Stoa of Attalos, 1949. During the 1949 season, work focused on clearing the area of the Stoa of Attalos in anticipation that the museum would be built there. This entailed removing many large architectural blocks. In addition exploratory excavations were begun in the area.

66. View from the Panathenaic Road looking south toward the Acropolis, 1949. On the left is the south end of the Stoa of Attalos and on the right in the middle foreground is the Church of the Holy Apostles before restoration.

Approach, Parking, etc. If the Stoa were to be used for Museum purposes it would be desirable to make it accessible from the Theseum Square by reconstituting the ancient east-to-west thoroughfare that passed just south of the Fountain House and South Stoa, bending it southward round the Church of the Holy Apostles that now overlies the east end of the South Stoa and so eastward past the Library of Pantainos. A small and inconspicuous parking lot might be arranged to the south of the Church and the Stoa Museum approached thence on foot.

General Advantages of the Project.

1. The site is ready and available, and its use would not involve the destruction of any ancient remains.

2. Adequate space would be provided for display, storage, office and workrooms.

3. The site would be exceedingly convenient for the completion of the current excavation and equally well placed for the eventual exploration of the Roman Market Place and the Library of Hadrian to the east.

4. The restoration would make intelligible to scholar and layman alike as nothing else possibly could a first rate example of Greek civic architecture.

5. The rebuilt Stoa would close the east side of the square, restoring to the Agora much of its ancient unity. Flanked on the east by the Stoa, on the west by Kolonos and the Hephaisteion, on the south by the Areopagus, the Athenian Agora would become one of the most impressive and attractive of all archaeological sites in Greece.

Homer A. Thompson Field Director, Agora Excavations
Athens, April 27, 1948

Dramatis Personae

Anastasios Orlandos	Department of Restoration of the Ministry of Education
Kostantinos Biris	Chairman of the Athens City Planning Commission
Ioannis Meliades	Ephor of Athens and the Acropolis
Ward H. Canaday	President of the Trustees
Charles Morgan	Chairman of the Managing Committee
John L. Caskey	Director of the American School of Classical Studies
Homer A. Thompson	Field Director, Agora Excavations
John Travlos	Architect, Agora Excavations
W. Stuart Thompson	Supervising Architect for the firm W. S. Thompson & Phelps Barnum
Georgios Biris	Consulting Engineer
Manuel A. Taverez	Supervising Engineer for the firm W. S. Thompson & Phelps Barnum

67. General view of the Agora looking north, 1949. Note remains of the Stoa of Attalos and the Church of the Holy Apostles on the right (east). The Old Excavation House complex is visible in the foreground.

68. General view of the Agora from the Hephaisteion, 1949. Compare this photograph with **2** and **5**.

A History Lesson: How Large a Stoa?

The history of the construction of the original Stoa of Attalos gradually became clear through study of the archaeological and architectural remains. Apparently the design of the Stoa of Attalos was altered several times during the course of its construction. The original plan was more modest in size with only fourteen shops along the eastern, back wall. The building was later extended to the south by another four shops. Eventually three more shops were added to the north. The reasons as to why and how the original building's design was altered so many times during its construction will never be known, but the history of its modern copy is more clear. On the next few pages are excerpts from correspondence between the principals involved with the reconstruction project.

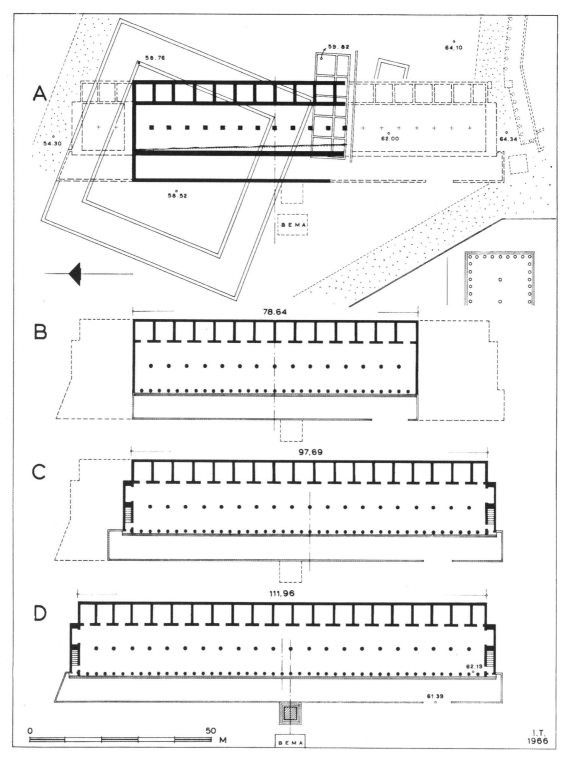

69. A drawing by John Travlos that illustrates the four phases of construction of the original Stoa of Attalos

Prologue to the Reconstruction

Correspondence between Homer A. Thompson and W. S. Thompson, 1952–1953

Homer A. Thompson cable to W. Stuart Thompson, March 22, 1952

"... we are all against a stair leading up to the terrace at the north end. Such did not exist in antiquity and we also feel that it would be well to limit access to the museum to the single ancient approach through the terrace parapet near its south end. At that point the approach is level, and many, probably most visitors will wish to enter the building only after completing a round of the excavation terrace."

Homer A. Thompson cable to W. Stuart Thompson, March 27, 1952

"Your design for basement acceptable but ramp ruled out by railway and exterior stair still considered undesirable. Revised sketches for upper story follow."

Homer A. Thompson letter to W. Stuart Thompson, March 28, 1952

"Stairways to the Top Floor. After long consideration of the advisability of inserting a 'grand stairway' at the middle of the building, we are still disposed to have the public reach the top floor by means of the ancient stairways at its ends. We fully realize that by modern standards the stairs are high and steep; they could be mitigated somewhat by the insertion of handrails. But they form an integral and interesting part of the ancient building and are so placed as to enable the visitor to cover the main floors and to enjoy the superb view from the upper floor with a minimum of walking. You will recall that even higher stairs stand between every visitor and the Acropolis, yet only a very small proportion of visitors are utterly discouraged."

Homer A. Thompson letter to W. Stuart Thompson, September 1, 1952

"I very much hope that we shall be able to do the full length of the building, for, in spite of the advantages which you point out in favor of the partial restoration, those of us on the spot are not enthusiastic. For one thing we have come to visualize the Stoa restored in toto as a most desirable and effective screen between the ancient and the modern."

Homer A. Thompson letter to W. Stuart Thompson, February 26, 1953

"It transpires from our archaeological study of the Stoa of Attalos that the original design envisaged a much shorter building, one which would have comprised only the middle 14 shops out of the 21 shops of the design as carried out. During construction the plan was extended northward by three shops (as we had previously known) and southward by four shops (as we have now discovered). John Travlos suggests that, if we are to restore only two thirds of the building, we should choose the part which would correspond with the original design. This suggestion appeals to me greatly inasmuch as it would leave the best preserved portions of the original superstructure open to inspection."

70. Drawing by W. S. Thompson illustrating the partial (two-thirds) reconstruction of the Stoa of Attalos

W. Stuart Thompson letter to Homer A. Thompson, March 4, 1953

"I quite agree with yours and Travlos suggestion that the building should be restored only for the middle fourteen shops. . . . I should strongly suggest that both end walls at each end of the fourteen be done in a temporary manner, building only the wall at the shop end and leaving the two end columns on each side as columns. . . . I am extremely happy about this discovery as I think this solution will make a very much better restoration artistically as it will show the center portion of the building and leave both ends of the building which are better preserved in situ."

Homer A. Thompson letter to W. Stuart Thompson, March 10, 1953

"This morning I went over the ground with Mr. Kostas Biris, Head of the City Planning Commission of Athens, and had a preliminary discussion with him about the new proposal. His initial reaction was unfavorable, his chief arguments being that it would leave the building without a head, that it would eliminate one of the most interesting and characteristic features of the Stoa, viz. its exterior stair, and that it would confuse more than it would help the visitor to grasp the original scheme of the building."

W. Stuart Thompson letter to Homer A. Thompson, March 17, 1953

"In thinking over his suggestion of the reconstruction of the middle fourteen rooms, I am very much inclined to agree with Mr. Kostas Biris that the reconstruction should be at the north end and that just building the central portion would not give a visitor any picture of the original building. It would just be a group of columns without the characteristic stair feature of the Stoa and we would have to build two gable ends that never existed. The more I think of the matter and visualize it from a quick sketch, the more I am convinced that we would be very greatly criticized for reconstructing the central portion only."

Homer A. Thompson letter to W. Stuart Thompson, April 11, 1953

"Professor Orlandos, who as you know is head of the Department of Restorations in the Ministry of Education and the man with whom we shall have most to do on the government side, assures me that he has succeeded by dint of a great effort in retaining this quarry [Akte, Piraeus] for the Stoa and he believes, since the quarrying conditions are good, that the stone could be gotten quickly. I had visited this quarry, among many others, last year and was favorably impressed by the quality of the stone and by the ready access to the quarry."

W. Stuart Thompson letter to Homer A. Thompson, May 15, 1953

"Mr. Canaday called me from Toledo yesterday and said that all formalities in America were now complete for the construction of the basement of the Stoa and probably the portion of the superstructure and the museum could be built within the amount of money available (approximately $900,000.00). He asked me to immediately proceed with the necessary construction drawings listing the materials necessary for the basement, etc."

Homer A. Thompson letter to W. Stuart Thompson, May 21, 1953

"This morning Jack Caskey and I called on Mr. Orlandos who was also pleased with the news. . . . Mr. Orlandos has repeatedly assured us that we need no further authorization for the start of work beyond his own approval as head of the Department of Restorations in the Ministry of Education, and this he is ready to give on receipt of an official request from the School which Jack Caskey is now submitting. . . . We are all looking forward with tremendous interest to the actual start of work on the Stoa which will so splendidly round off the Agora project and which should mean so much to the relations between the two countries."

W. Stuart Thompson letter to Homer A. Thompson, May 25, 1953

"I too am very pleased that your dream of the reconstruction of the Stoa of Attalos is at last about to take concrete form. . . . I hope that the Piraeus stone quarry can be opened quickly and stone actually received on the job in the shortest possible space of time. I also think it very wise to take Mr. Orlandos advise about how to get the work started and to get the stone at the earliest possible moment."

71. In 1948, a full reconstruction of the Stoa of Attalos was proposed.

72. When the Trustees of the American School tentatively approved the construction of the Agora museum in 1952, only a two-thirds reconstruction (from the north end) was considered financially possible. The southern third of the building would have been left unfinished until funds for a full reconstruction could be raised.

73. During the spring of 1953, a two-thirds reconstruction of the Stoa of Attalos in the central portion of the building's original footprint was briefly considered. This proposal, quickly abandoned for aesthetic and practical reasons, would have left the ancient walls of the north and south ends alone.

THE STOA AND ITS RECONSTRUCTION

The Stoa of Attalos was originally built by King Attalos II of Pergamon (159–138 B.C.) as a gift to the Athenians in appreciation of the time he spent in Athens studying under the philosopher Karneades. What he gave the city was an elaborate stoa, a large two-storeyed double colonnade with rows of shops behind the colonnades. The building was made of local materials, marble for the facade and columns, and limestone for the walls; it measures 116 meters long and had 42 shops in all. The stoa became the major commercial building or shopping center in the Agora and was used for centuries, from its construction in around 150 B.C. until its destruction at the hands of the Herulians in A.D. 267. It was chosen to serve as the museum because it was large enough and because enough architectural elements were preserved to allow an accurate reconstruction; in addition, as noted, the northern end stood to the original roof line, allowing precision in recreating the height of the building.

The building was reerected between 1953 and 1956. Quarries in Piraeus and on Mt. Penteli were opened so as to provide material similar to the original. As many as 150 workmen were employed, including 50 master masons, 20 carpenters, and 5 steelworkers. Where possible, remains of the original building were incorporated: the north end, the southernmost shops, part of the south wall, and the south end of the outer steps. Elsewhere the modern reconstruction rests on the original foundations and is an almost exact replica of the ancient building, with representative pieces of the original included in order to allow the visitor a chance to check the validity of the reconstruction for him- or herself. The ground floor is given over to public display, sculpture and large marbles in the colonnades, small objects in a long gallery consisting of ten of the original shops. The first floor is used for the excavation offices, workrooms, and archives as well as for additional storage. More storerooms were created in basements at foundation level. Dedicated on the 3rd of September, 1956, the Stoa of Attalos celebrates its 50th anniversary as the Agora museum in 2006.

The reconstruction leads the visitor to appreciate why stoas were such a common form of public building among the Greeks, used in agoras, sanctuaries, near theaters, and wherever many people were expected to gather. The spacious colonnades provided shelter for literally thousands of people, protecting them from sun in summer and wind and rain in winter, while allowing in abundant light and fresh air.

74. Drawing by the early traveler Edward Dodwell showing the northeast corner of the Stoa of Attalos in 1805

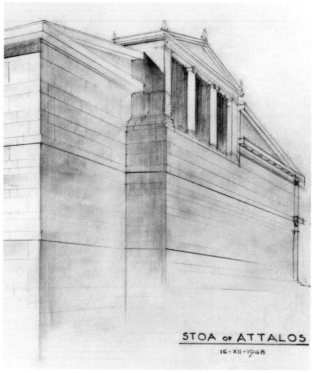

75. Drawing by John Travlos showing a proposed reconstruction of the northeast corner of the Stoa of Attalos, 1948

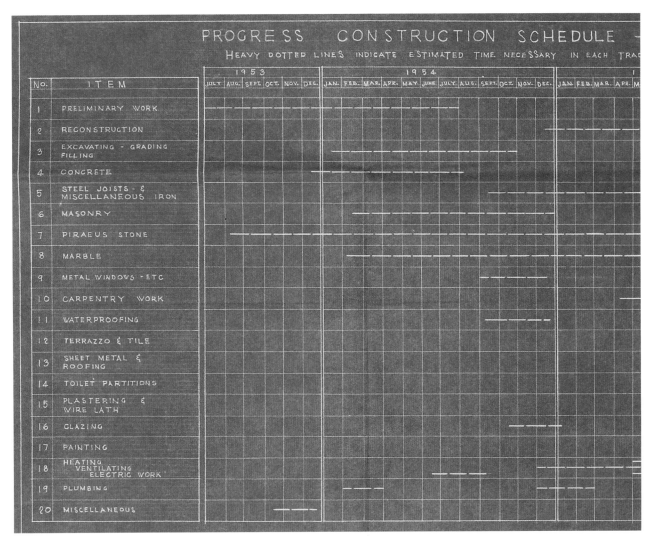

76. Detail of the construction schedule prepared by W. S. Thompson in 1953, with a three-year timeline for completing the two-thirds reconstruction of the Stoa of Attalos

In May of 1953 the Trustees of the American School formally approved funding for a two-thirds reconstruction of the Stoa of Attalos and work commenced immediately. The construction timetable made by W. S. Thompson (**76**) illustrates the broad categories of work to be done and the proposed schedule of the project based on a three-year timeline.

Work commenced in the deep northern foundations and proceeded south. The foundations of the original building were the focus of the initial work of the project. Prior archaeological excavations had revealed an alarming amount of water flowing through the area and this caused great concern because it was feared that water had weakened the poros limestone foundations. Although the new museum would be primarily supported with a reinforced concrete superstructure, the original foundations would contribute significantly to holding up the building and had to be strengthened. Also, the area had to be dry since a basement storage area was to be constructed in between the deepest foundations to house the immense amount of excavated material.

The chart also shows graphically how, after a few months of preliminary work, many different trades were at the site working on all aspects of the project. Anastasios Orlandos and John Travlos, with the assistance of M. Kourouniotes and A. Stavroudes, were responsible for making sure the reconstruction duplicated the original design of the building as closely as possible. Georgios Biris, a civil engineer, was responsible for the concrete structural design.

During the summer and fall of 1953, a solution to the water problem was found, the foundations were strengthened, and finally construction of the basement began. Thereafter the pace of work intensified and many things began to happen at the same time. All of this work was coordinated by Manuel A. Taverez, who was the supervising engineer for the reconstruction project. Christophoros Zotos was charged with paying salaries and keeping track of the multitude of expenses on site.

FINDING THE BUILDING BLOCKS

Even before the final decision to reconstruct the Stoa of Attalos was reached, considerable effort was devoted to finding sources of poros limestone and marble suitable for the project. Anastasios Orlandos offered to open a quarry for the poros limestone at Akte in Piraeus, and work began there in June of 1953. Soon after, another quarry was engaged at Drapetsona, on the opposite side of Piraeus, when it became apparent the Akte quarry could not produce enough stone. At the same time sources for the white and blue marble were being investigated in quarries on Penteli. The amount of stone needed was so great that contracts with several quarries were signed to guarantee delivery to meet the project's timetable. Eventually 1,050 cubic meters of poros limestone and 650 cubic meters of marble were quarried, worked, and installed for the reconstruction of the Stoa of Attalos. The dollar to drachma exchange rate in September of 1953 was approximately $1 = 30,000 drachmas. The price of Dionysos marble delivered to the Agora work site was approximately $100 per cubic meter. Poros stone was slightly cheaper at 2,500,000 drachmas or approximately $83 per cubic meter.

77. Marble quarry in Dionysos, 1951. Left to right: Homer A. Thompson, John L. Caskey, Ward H. Canaday, and probably one of the Argyroudis brothers.

"Conference this morning in office of A. Kyriakides with the two Argyroudis brothers of the [Dionyso-]*Penteli Marble Co., J. Travlos & H.A.T. present. We had submitted to this company a list of priorities for the supply of the marble, the latest to be delivered within 2 years of signing the agreement. The brothers regard this as a practical basis for discussion but insist that the whole lot cannot be supplied in less than 3 years. They undertake to draft a formal reply to our last proposal & to submit it for dispatch to W.S. Thompson"* (Nb. ΣA XVII, p. 3,240; July 23, 1953).

"After long negotiations we came to an agreement with the Dionyso-Pentelikon Marble Co. to supply us with marble, for a period of 3 months, as much as 60 cu. m. & more if they could, at 3,000,000 dr. per cu. m. delivered. At the end of the 3 months both sides will review the situation & consider what to do next. The company claims to be hard at work on our order but has not as yet delivered any marble" (Nb. ΣA XVII, p. 3,268; September 16, 1953).

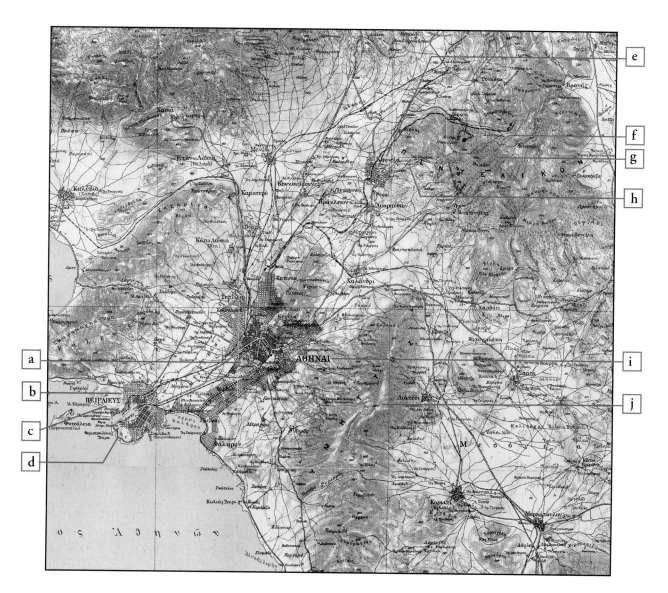

78. Map of Attica (dated 1923) showing the sources of poros limestone in Piraeus and the locations of marble quarries on Mount Penteli: (**a**) the Agora; (**b**) the city of Piraeus; (**c**) the area of Piraeus called Drapetsona, where the second poros quarry was located; (**d**) the peninsula of Piraeus named Akte, where the first poros quarry was opened; (**e**) the village of Kifissia (now a suburb of Athens), through which one must pass to get to the marble quarries on the north and south slopes of Mount Penteli; (**f**) the village of Dionysos, near the Dionyso-Pentelikon Co. marble quarry; (**g**) Mount Penteli; (**h**) the area of Mount Penteli known as Kokinarras, where the Parthenon Marble Co. had its quarry; (**i**) the city of Athens; (**j**) Mount Hymettos. The distance from the Agora to Piraeus is ca. 8 kilometers, and to the marble quarries on Mount Penteli ca. 20 kilometers.

"*Inasmuch as the Dionyso-Pentelikon Co. showed little disposition to help us further in finding dark marble of suitable quality & color, we call in Mr. Kaloudis of the Parthenon Marble Co. & after a couple of preliminary conferences we agree to take blue marble from him at the prices fixed in his price list + 20%. He had previously submitted several samples the color of which was adjudged to be satisfactory. His quarry is situated in the Kokkinara district above Kiphissia.*

He took our catalogue of sizes & agreed to work as closely as possible to them. It was agreed however that we should accept large blocks which would work out as multiples of certain members, these to be delivered to the commercial marble saw to be cut to size, the rest to be delivered at the stoa.

Mr. Kaloudis refused to commit himself as to rate of production.

He promised to save for us any white marble that might seem suitable to our needs but pointed out that his quarry yielded little white" (Nb. ΣA XVII, pp. 3,300–3,301; March 10, 1954).

79. Ancient quarry cuttings in the poros limestone quarry at Akte, Piraeus, 1953

80:a, b *(below)*. Moving blocks by hand and jack in Akte quarry, 1953

81 *(below)*. Remains of ancient poros quarry visible above modern quarry at Akte, 1953

82. Roughing out blocks by hand at Akte quarry, 1953

83. John Travlos and Homer Thompson checking blocks in Akte quarry, 1953

84:a, b *(right)*. The difficulties encountered in moving the building stones were considerable.

"The first blocks are ready to be picked up on July 4. We arrange with our hauling contractor, Polychronis Kakouris, to transport the stone at a rate of 220,000 [drachmas] per load, we to do loading & unloading & putting on as much as the truck will carry. We send down one of our old cranes to be kept in the quarry & bring up the other crane from Piraeus for use in the excavation. Sophokles Lekkas goes down with his own picked crew to attend to loading for the first few trips. Soon we send down only one of our old experienced workmen who calls on the quarry workmen to assist him. We soon find that offloading is more dangerous than loading; at first we simply dump the load by tilting the truck body, letting the blocks slide together to the ground. Several have broken & we must devise other methods" (Nb. ΣA XVII, p. 3,228).

85. Quarrying marble in Dionysos, 1955

86. Moving blocks with crane in Dionysos quarry, 1955

87:a, b. Shaping and splitting blocks of marble in Dionysos quarry, 1955

88. Lifting and stacking marble blocks in Dionysos quarry, 1955

89. Inspecting a worked poros block, June 1953. Left to right: John Travlos, Mastoras Kostas, and Kostas's nephew, Stelios.

"Mastora Kostas, despite his 84 [sic] years has quickly organized his force of stone cutters. Starting on June 8 with but a single technician, viz. his nephew [Stelios] he had taken on 15 technicians by the middle of July, adding them gradually. . . . Mastora Kostas receives 4,500,000 [drachmas] monthly ($150). The technicians have been occupied thus far in cutting the poros blocks for the Stoa terrace wall, leaving "lifting bosses" as in the ancient stones & matching the ancient surface as closely as possible. We have gradually improved working accommodations for the stone cutters. Starting with a small vertical screen of galvanized iron that cast a shadow large enough to protect two men at the most, we next erected a simple shed with 4 posts supporting a few sheets of galvanized iron under which a half dozen men might sit" (Nb. ΣA XVII, pp. 3,230–3,232).

90. Stone cutter working a poros block. Approximately 1,050 cubic meters of poros limestone were used in the reconstruction project.

91. Modern stone-working tools used to work the stone and marble blocks for the Stoa of Attalos reconstruction

92. An Ionic capital (either single or double) took 45 work-days to complete. An Ionic column (base, shaft, and capital) was estimated to cost $700 for materials and labor.

93. A Doric capital took 18 work-days to finish. The cost of the material and labor of a Doric column (shaft, capital, and fluting) was estimated at $1,000.

94. An upper cornice block with lion's head took 50 work-days to finish.

95. Drilling a block of white marble from Dionysos in preparation for splitting it into two smaller pieces. An entry in the notebook records the block's dimensions and weight:

1.00 × 1.35 × 3.10 m =
  4.185 cubic meters

4.185 × 2,800 kilograms =
  11.718 metric tons

96. Stacks of roughly shaped blocks in marble yard waiting to be worked. In total, over 650 cubic meters of white and blue marble were used for the stoa reconstruction.

97. A 60 cm diamond-toothed stone-cutting saw was purchased and installed. Rough cut blocks from the quarry were cut onsite to the dimensions needed, thus requiring less work by the stone cutters to finish and speeding up production of the stone needed to build the stoa.

98. Marble workers using a time-tested method of working marble: working the stone by hand. Air-driven tools were tried but the stone cutters preferred working the stone as their ancient predecessors had.

Letter from Manuel A. Taverez to W. S. Thompson, May 18, 1954

"As for the use of air tools, trials have been made and my preliminary observation is that these tools only have a limited use. The situation is conditioned by the following reasons:

a. None of the rippers or cleaning up chisels produce the tooled effect desired on the marble surface.

b. During handling of the air hammer, considerable vibration is present which makes it difficult for the operator to control. The finish is therefore rather uneven and would require sanding down to obtain a level surface. I believe that where sanded surfaces are called for, the air hammer would be perfectly satisfactory, altho, and this may seem odd, slower than hand tooling.

c. To prove the previous point, we set up one block and had two men start out at one end, and not to be facetious, the man with the hand tool won by six hand lengths over the air hammer operator.

d. The only tool which has shown definite advantages in air hammer work is the four point tooth chisel for roughing down the surface to where the mason can easily finish the block with a ripper and cleaning chisel. However, heavy needle chiseling is required first before the tooth chisel can be employed as the air hammer weight in blows does not match a mason's arm force.

We are still continuing to experiment and check the air hammer methods, but aside, some of the older men snort at the thought of using the air tools, and in some cases they are right in stating that control of the hand hammer is surer and certain when finishing marble. I will advise you further when we have given the air hammers thorough testing."

99. Some of the marble work was done by subcontractors. Column capitals and bases are being cut by contract in the marble-working shop of Theodoros Mastoris near the First Cemetery, Athens, April 11, 1955.

100. Digging a trench and laying drainage pipe behind the stoa, 1953

101. Foundation walls at the north end of the stoa, which extend approximately 8 meters below ground. The basement of the museum was built within these deep walls.

102. Beginning construction of the front terrace wall on the northwestern corner of the stoa

103. On the left, men are digging a trench beneath the foundations so that the underpinning of the bottom course of stones can be poured for the shop front wall. Partially finished piers of the ground-floor slab are visible on the right.

104. *"In order to make sure of a solid bedding for the concrete wall that will support the main Doric order we have had to strip away a good many of the conglomerate blocks which were found in place in this foundation: a couple of courses opposite Piers 12–19, one course opposite Piers 7–10. In the latter region we shall also have to remove, alas, the one row, single course, of heavy conglomerate blocks which supported the Stoa gutter; they were set close against the W. face of the main foundation"* (Nb. ΣA XVII, p. 3,344; May 21, 1954).

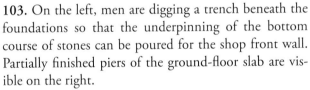

105. While the front terrace and back walls were being constructed, the basement piers were poured to a height to receive the ground-floor slab. Visible in this photograph are the finished basement piers. The large piers at the left will bear the inner colonnade. The smaller piers will support the ground-floor and terrace slabs.

STEEL AND CONCRETE

The steel reinforcing bars used in the concrete were manufactured by Bethlehem Steel Co. of Bethlehem, Pennsylvania. The decision to ship the steel from America was practical. First of all, finding enough steel in Greece just after World War II was difficult, so importing it ensured the supply of this essential building material; secondly, the steel was of a type not yet produced in Greece.

Letter from W. S. Thompson to Charles H. Morgan, March 17, 1952

"I am enclosing a copy of a report from our Consulting Engineer, Charles Mayer, dated March 14th, 1952. As you will see from this report, the present design shown by Mr. Biris is economical and should not be changed. The only change which he would suggest is if reinforcing steel is sent from America that we send deformed bars in place of the round rods shown in Mr. Biris drawings, as the stresses could then be increased 50% and a corresponding 50% savings be made in the purchase of the steel. As you know deformed bars are only used in the United States and are not used in Europe."

106. Steel workers installing reinforcing bars for the ground-floor concrete slab above the basement, August 1954

107. Workmen preparing forms to pour the ground-floor concrete slab over the east basement storeroom. On the left, construction of the back and front shop walls proceeds above ground-floor level. View looking south, August 1954.

108. A storage shed was built in the front middle portion of the stoa to store tools and the cement produced by the Herakles Cement Company. Adjacent to the shed a mechanical mixer was placed and a tower was built with an elevator to lift the mixed concrete to the level of each storey. Sand and gravel were brought in and dumped in the yard near the mixer and then shoveled into the mixer to make each batch. The mixer was capable of making approximately one-fifth of a cubic meter of wet concrete per batch.

Georgios Moutaphis was awarded a contract in September of 1953 as the concrete subcontractor. Moutaphis provided the machinery, tools, labor, and oversight of mixing and pouring the concrete, and the American School provided the wood for the forms, steel, cement, sand, and gravel. The average cost of a finished cubic meter of concrete was estimated to be approximately $30. Over 4,400 cubic meters of concrete were mixed onsite.

109. Georgios Biris, pictured in the center, was the civil engineer responsible for the design of all the concrete construction. Here, Biris is supervising pouring the first portion of the upper storey floor slab. The wet concrete would sometimes have been transported to the area in wheelbarrows, but most often it was carried by workmen in 20-liter tins (ca. 5 U.S. gallons). To pour a cubic meter of cement would require at least 50 tins.

GROUND FLOOR

110. General view of the stoa reconstruction from the southeast. Visible on the right is the wooden scaffold erected along the back wall and workers setting poros limestone blocks, April 12, 1954.

"We have today completed the restoration of this wall [the stoa's back wall] up to the ancient floor level of the shops, i.e. to the level of the bottom of the orthostates. It had been broken down to the deepest opposite Shops XVIII–XX where we have had to replace 6 courses below the orthostates. We are backing the wall with reinforced concrete in all the part below the ancient floor level; above this we plan to use rubble stone backing" (Nb. ΣA XVII, p. 3,316).

111:a, b *(above and right).* Setting orthostates in rear wall

"This week we began setting the large poros orthostates in the back wall of the Stoa. The blocks are brought in from the north by railway & the larger ones are then placed with the half of a crane which takes hold of a lewis in the top of the block. Each block is fastened to the course below by means of an end dowel made from a piece of 3/4 inch reinforcing rod set in cement. The orthostates are kept in line with one another by a packing of mortar in a common groove between adjacent ends. They are tied to the backing of rubble stone by means of iron clamps" (Nb. ΣA XVII, p. 3,339; May 6, 1954).

112. At the north end of the stoa (upper left) plywood forms are being placed to pour the concrete slab over the terrace storeroom. Concrete underpinning is being poured for the front steps of the stoa south of the basement storeroom. The area of the stoa south of the basement storerooms is being levelled in preparation to pour the floor slab. The back wall of the stoa has been raised through the string course above the orthostates and backed with cement, June 16, 1954.

113. View looking north along the entire length of the stoa. In the foreground, work is progressing on the terrace gutter and steps. In the background, the finished concrete slabs over the terrace basement and the east basement are visible. On the right, wooden scaffolding has been erected for work on the back wall of the stoa, August 1954.

114. The back wall of the stoa rebuilt to the course ready to receive the window lintels, August 16, 1954

SETTING THE FIRST COLUMNS

By November of 1954, stone cutters had been hard at work for 16 months carving the capitals, bases, and drums. The first column to be erected was an Ionic column of the inner colonnade. Drawing from the stockpile of finished pieces (116), work proceeded quickly; columns of both the inner and outer colonnades of the ground floor were erected, starting from the southern end of the building and working north.

115. Column drums being shaped in the marble shed

116. Finished capitals and bases on storage shelves

117. Scaffold placed to erect the first column. The bottom drum has been set and workmen are in the process of setting the second drum.

118. The first complete column erected, November 11, 1954. Work began immediately to erect the second.

119. Loading a finished column drum onto a rail cart in the marble yard

120. Workmen pushing the column drum by rail cart to the front of the stoa where it will be set

121. Lifting the column drum into an upright position

122. By December of 1954, eight Doric and two Ionic columns of the ground-floor colonnade had been set in the central portion of the stoa.

61

The Full Reconstruction Approved

During the fall of 1954, Manuel Taverez and W. S. Thompson corresponded regarding the escalating costs of the stoa project. Prices for labor and raw materials had increased rapidly since the project began, and this seemed certain to continue. As a full reconstruction of the stoa was ultimately envisioned, it was determined that savings could be made by expanding the construction project immediately, extending contracts for the basic materials and keeping the skilled workforce engaged. Thus, in January of 1955, the Trustees of the American School authorized the complete reconstruction of the Stoa of Attalos.

123. View of the stoa from the southwest, February 11, 1955

124. View of the southern portion of the stoa from behind the building looking southwest toward the Areopagus, February 11, 1955. Aside from stabilizing the walls little work had been done to the southern part of the building. Both photographs (**123, 124**) illustrate how much of the stoa had been completed during the first 18 months and how much still had to be built!

N²	ITEMS	1953	1954	1955	1956	1957
		JUL AUG SEP OCT NOV DEC	JAN FEB MAR APR MAY JUN JUL AUG SEP OCT NOV DEC	JAN FEB MAR APR MAY JUN JUL AUG SEP OCT NOV DEC	JAN FEB MAR APR MAY JUN JUL AUG SEP OCT NOV DEC	JAN FEB MAR APR MAY JUN
1	PRELIMIN WORK					
2	RECONSTRUCTION					
3	EXCAV. GRADING, FILLING					
4	CONCRETE					
5	MISC. IRON					
6	MASONRY					
7	PIRAEUS STONE					
8	MARBLE					
9	METAL WINDOWS ETC.					
10	CARPENTRY WORK					
11	WATERPROOFING					
12	TERRAZZO & TILE					
13	SHEET MET. & ROOFING					
14	TOILET PARTITIONS					
15	PLASTERING & LATHING					
16	GLAZING					
17	PAINTING					
18	HEAT, VENT. & ELEC. WORK					
19	PLUMBING					
20	MISCELLANEOUS					

PROGRESS CONSTRUCTION SCHEDULE – STOA OF ATTALOS – ATHENS, GREECE

HEAVY LINES INDICATE ESTIMATED TIME NECESSARY IN EACH TRADE: CONSTRUCTION STARTED JULY 1, 1953 – ESTIM. COMPLETION NOV. 30, 1956

ATHENS, GREECE - DEC. 1954

125. A revised construction schedule for the project. The green line (added) indicates the approximate halfway point when the decision was made to carry out a complete reconstruction. When Canaday authorized the full reconstruction he did so with the hope that the building would be ready by September of 1956, when the Trustees of the American School were scheduled to come to Athens to celebrate the American School's 75th anniversary. At the beginning of the project, W. S. Thompson estimated that the original two-thirds reconstruction would be finished by late 1956, but suddenly the final third of the building was added to the project and the completion date advanced by three months! The red line (added) illustrates the month when the stoa would be dedicated, and the space between the green and red lines shows the considerable amount of work still to do before the dedication ceremonies.

126. The workmen of the stoa project pause on March 22, 1955, for a group photograph, perhaps celebrating their accomplishments. By this date nine shop doorways, six Ionic columns (inner colonnade), and sixteen Doric columns (outer colonnade), along with part of the Doric entablature, had been set.

DEADLINE: 18 MONTHS

Letter from Ward M. Canaday to Homer A. Thompson, February 12, 1955

"I know of nothing now that has not been cleared completely for going ahead with the utmost steam we can put in the boiler and I shall look forward with the greatest interest to have word from you."

127. April 28, 1955. View of the north basement storeroom. The modern poured concrete and ancient stone piers of the building are clearly visible. While work on the upper storeys continued, the basement storage area was finished. Wooden shelving was installed and objects and context pottery from the Old Excavation House began to be transferred.

128. May 11, 1955. Pouring the first portion of the upper-storey slab. Working from the south to the north, sections of the upper-storey slab are poured as soon as the outer and inner colonnade and the shop walls are ready. View looking northeast.

129. June 5, 1955. Pouring the second section of the upper-storey slab. In the foreground, scaffold surrounds an inner colonnade column being erected. The back and front shop walls are ready for the next section of the upper-storey slab. View looking south.

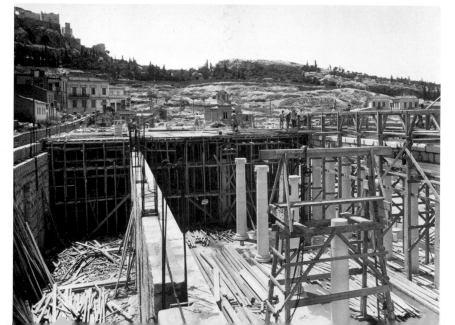

130. July 14, 1955. Fluting the first Doric column.

"The reconstruction has been illuminating for many of the technical aspects of ancient construction, not least for the fluting of the columns. In keeping with the normal practice in stoas only the outer row of columns was fluted on each floor, since only they could profit fully from the sun. The front columns of the upper storey being comparatively short are monolithic so that they can be more easily fluted before rather than after setting. The shafts of the lower front columns, on the other hand, are built up each of three drums. If these drums had been channeled individually before erection superhuman care would have been required to assure exact alignment. The solution adopted by the ancients and followed by the modern restorers is to start the fluting before setting at top and bottom and to complete it after setting. For this operation the marble cutters have worked in teams of four per column. The first column required ca. 76 man-days of labor for the fluting alone and the cost came to a little over 9,000 drachmai or $300; with experience the time and cost per unit have been somewhat reduced" (H. A. Thompson, "Activities in the Athenian Agora: 1955," *Hesperia* 25 [1956], p. 68).

131 *(below).* August 16, 1955. Setting the Doric entablature at the north end of the stoa. The inner and outer colonnades of the ground floor had reached the north end of the building by this date.

132 *(below).* September 27, 1955. Lowering the keystone of the arch of the northern exedra.

133. October 10, 1955.
The first load of roof tiles was delivered. Pictured here are workmen in the Kriton Deleveres factory (located in Piraeus) making pan tiles. The tiles on the shelves behind the workmen are drying before being fired. Approximately 5,000 pan tiles (ca. 0.55 × 0.74 m) and 5,000 cover tiles were made by special order, duplicating the dimensions of their ancient counterparts, to cover the roof of the stoa (ca. 116 meters × 20 meters = ca. 2,300 square meters of roof).

134. November 16, 1955.
Moving tins of context pottery from the Old Excavation House to new storage in the basement of the stoa.

135. December 19, 1955.
Stoa colonnade with arch over northern exedra has been completed. Rail tracks have been laid inside the ground-floor colonnade to move marble blocks. The colonnade became a work space for the marble cutters as soon as the scaffolds were removed. A balustrade block rests on workbenches in the bottom left foreground. Rough shaped pieces of numerous other architectural elements are lying on the floor ready to be worked.

136. Christmas 1955.

The workmen gather for a group photograph in December. In the foreground, cornice blocks and antefixes rest on the terrace wall. Workmen will begin in two months time to set these architectural pieces on the upper cornice of the facade.

137. January 3, 1956.

The first six Pergamene columns of the inner colonnade of the upper storey have been set.

138. February 13, 1956.

Working on the back of the Ionic epistyle. Work on the entablature followed close behind the setting of the double Ionic columns of the upper storey's outer colonnade.

139. March 8, 1956.
The point at which the northern two-thirds of the building meets the southern third. Because the stoa is so long (ca. 116 m), expansion joints like this one were incorporated in the modern reconstruction to accommodate thermal expansion and contraction of the building. This photograph was taken from on top of the front shop wall looking north. The view gives an impression of the cross-section of the stoa from the ground-floor colonnade to the roof.

140. April 11, 1956.
General view of the progress of the reconstruction. Sections of the roof of the stoa are being poured. In the bottom right, work on the restoration of the Church of the Holy Apostles is nearing completion.

141. May 24, 1956.
Cornice and sima at the northwest corner of the building have been set in preparation to pour the roof slab.

142. June 1956.
Originally, the concrete beams supporting the upper storey were to be left exposed and painted. Instead, laminated wood pieces were installed surrounding the concrete beams to give the impression of the ancient construction. The laminated beams were made from Western Douglas Fir and manufactured by the Rilco Laminated Products Co. of St. Paul, Minnesota.

143. July 1956.
Polishing the marble terrazzo floor in the lower colonnade.

144. August 1956.
Laying the roof tiles. The western half of the roof, visible to the public, would be nearly complete on the day of the dedication. The eastern half would be finished soon after.

145 *(above)*. August 1956. The large statue of Apollo Patroos, found by the Archaeological Society at Athens in their excavations of 1907 and stored at the National Archaeological Museum, was returned to the Agora in August and erected in the stoa.

146 *(above)*. September 1956. The finished south end of the stoa at the time of the dedication. Clearly visible are the ancient stones that have been incorporated into the reconstruction of the building. The parapet has been painted as it was in ancient times.

147 *(below)*. The "Law against Tyranny" inscription (I 6524) was also erected in the colonnade before the dedication ceremony.

148 *(below)*. The north end of the stoa showing the finished outer staircase

149. September 1956. The stoa and the northeast side of the Agora as they looked at the time of the dedication ceremony. The construction debris has been removed and areas backfilled. Some large architectural pieces have been placed for display along the terrace wall. Soon the planting of trees and shrubs will transform the area into a landscaped archaeological park. The buildings in the foreground would remain for several more months until the project was completed.

150. September 3, 1956. John L. Caskey, Director of the American School, delivering his remarks at the dedication ceremony. Homer A. Thompson, Field Director of the Agora Excavations, Pausanias S. Katsotas, Mayor of Athens, Ray L. Thurston, Chargé d'Affaires of the American Embassy, and Ward M. Canaday, President of the Board of Trustees of the School, all spoke at the opening ceremony. Afterward, the King and Queen of Greece dedicated the opening of the museum and a reception followed.

151. The overflow crowds lining the terrace on the day of the dedication of the stoa

THE MUSEUM COLLECTION

On display in the public galleries of the stoa is a selection of the thousands of objects recovered in the past 75 years, reflecting the use of the area from 3000 B.C. to A.D. 1500. Most significant perhaps, is the material—unique to the site—illustrating the mechanics of the world's first attested democracy. This material includes ostraka (inscribed potsherds) (**154**), used as ballots to exile over-ambitious politicians; allotment machines (**155**) and bronze identification tags (**157**), used in selecting an Athenian jury; and clay tokens (**156**) and inscribed lead strips, used in the administration of the Athenian cavalry.

Context is essential in understanding archaeological material. The great museums of Europe and the United States often display magnificent objects with little or no information as to where they were found and what else was found with them. What sets the Agora project and museum apart from most collections is the relationship of the objects to the archives. Because the excavations began so late, a generation or more after other large-scale digs in the Mediterranean (Pompeii, Ostia, Knossos, Dephi, Olympia, Pergamon, Ephesos, and Priene, to name a few), the same record-keeping system adopted at the beginning has been used to the present day, supplemented of course by new technology. This means that every object found in the Agora excavations is stored in the Stoa of Attalos, together with the record of its recovery. The inventory is large: 35,000 pieces of pottery, 7,600 inscriptions, 3,500 pieces of sculpture, 5,000 architectural fragments, 6,000 lamps, 15,000 stamped amphora handles, and over 70,000 coins. This vast collection has all been entered into a unified database, part of a collaborative project with the Packard Humanities Institute. Because of this correlation of objects and archives, the museum collection serves as a center for archaeological research, used every year by hundreds of scholars from all over the world.

152 *(above)* & **153** *(below)*. August 14, 1956. Installation of the museum exhibition began in mid-August. In the photograph above, Eugene Vanderpool, a member of the staff, and his daughter Anne, one of many who volunteered their time to help bring the project to completion, are seen working on one of the first cases to be installed.

154. Ostraka of the Athenian generals Alkibiades and Nikias, both candidates for ostracism in 417–415 B.C. (P 29373, P 31179, Agora Museum)

155. Fragment of an allotment machine (kleroterion), probably used in the Council House (in the period when there were 12 tribes) for the selection of committees representing all the tribes except that holding the presidency. Bronze tickets similar to **157** would have been inserted in the slots, which are clearly visible in the photograph. On the left side of the stone can be seen the holes for an attachment, a mechanical device that would have made the selection by chance (I 3967, Agora Museum).

156 *(right).* Clay tokens or passports of a border commander, 4th century B.C. (SS 8080, MC 1245, Agora Museum)

157 *(below).* Bronze juror's ticket (pinakion), 4th century B.C. This identification ticket carries the juror's name, Demophanes, the first letters of his father's name, Phili[- - -], and his deme, Kephesia (B 822, Agora Museum).

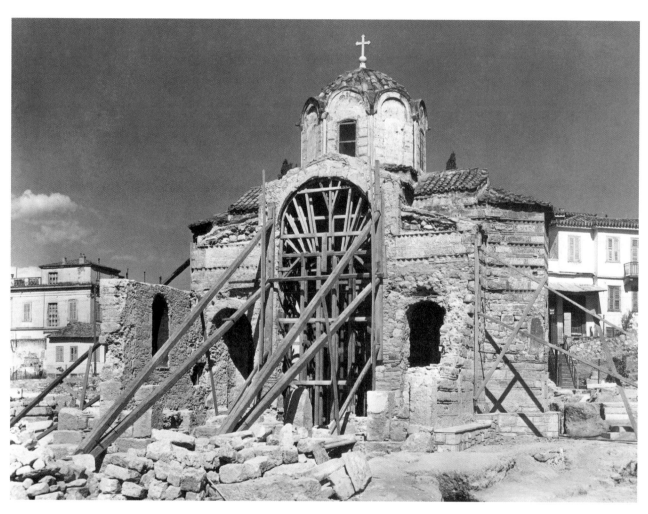

158. View of the Church of the Holy Apostles from the southwest, August 1954, after demolition of the later additions had been completed

THE CHURCH OF THE HOLY APOSTLES
RESTORATION

159. View of the restored Church of the Holy Apostles from the southwest, April 2006

THE CHURCH OF THE HOLY APOSTLES

Though several churches were removed in the clearing of the site for excavation, it was decided to save and restore the little Byzantine church dedicated to the Holy Apostles. The church, with an unusual tetraconch interior plan and decorative tilework on the exterior, is among the oldest in Athens, probably to be dated just before A.D. 1000. It was surely the focal point of an extensive neighborhood in the Byzantine period, the remains of which were recorded and removed in the course of the excavations. The eastern half of the church was relatively untouched, but several additions, the latest dating to the late 19th century, had damaged and obscured the western end. After excavation, these later additions were removed and the church restored to its original form. The work was funded by the Samuel H. Kress Foundation and supervised by Alison Frantz. With the Stoa of Attalos, this restoration was completed and dedicated in 1956. The festival of the Twelve Apostles is still celebrated at the church every June 30th.

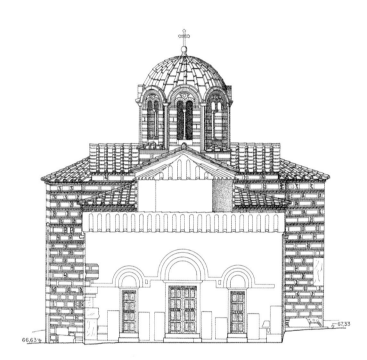

160. Western elevation of the Church of the Holy Apostles prior to restoration. Drawing by William B. Dinsmoor Jr. (W.B.D. Jr.)

161. William B. Dinsmoor Jr., Architect of the Agora Excavations, 1967–1988

W.B.D., JR. - 1969

162. Southern elevation of the Church of the Holy Apostles, prior to restoration. Drawing by W.B.D. Jr.

76

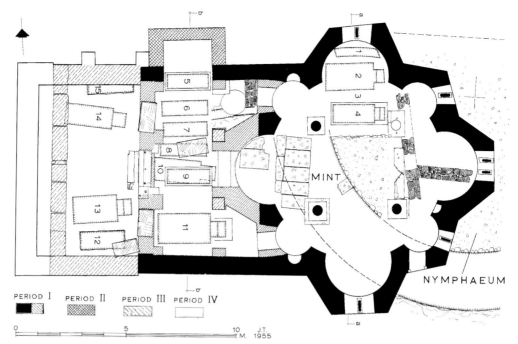

NYMPHAEUM

MINT

PERIOD I   PERIOD II   PERIOD III   PERIOD IV

0   5   10   J.T.
M.   1955

163 *(above).* Period plan showing the original layout of the church (Period I); the three successive alterations to its design; the 15 tombs beneath the floor; and the pre-Christian archaeological features, the Mint and the Nymphaeum. Drawing by W.B.D. Jr.

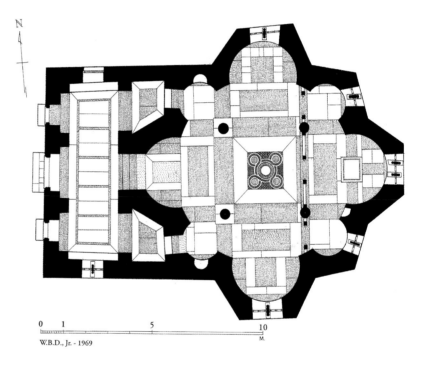

N

0   1   5   10
M.
W.B.D., Jr. - 1969

164. Restored plan of the original layout of the church, showing its unusual tetraconch design. Drawing by W.B.D. Jr.

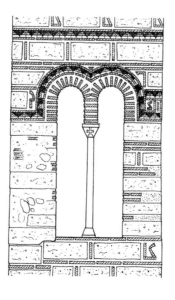

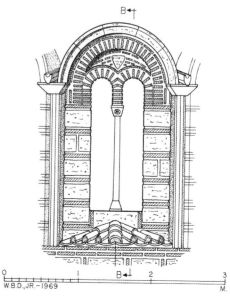

B

0   B   2   3
M.
W.B.D., JR.-1969

165. Detail of windows illustrating the decorative tilework. Drawing by W.B.D. Jr.

166. View of the north side of the church in 1953, before restoration. The bell tower and the considerable alterations to the narthex on the west side are clearly visible.

"On February 12, 1954, the Department of Antiquities of the Ministry of Education approved the request for permission to demolish the modern addition to the Church of the Holy Apostles, with a view to restoring the church in its original form. On February 22 two workmen began stripping the plaster from the walls to determine the extent of the original walls. Good Byzantine masonry, similar to that of the eastern part of the church was exposed on the lower part of the north wall as far as the door and bell tower. The original length of this wall is so far unclear. The south wall seems to have suffered at least one major destruction, and from a point ca. 2 m. west of the southern apse little original masonry remains above the lower course. There is so far no trace of early work west of the door on either side" (Nb. HA I, p. 2).

167. View of the southeast corner of the church, April 30, 1952. Note the windows of the dome, which have been altered or closed by masonry.

168. View of the west end of the church, February 25, 1952. On the right, workmen are beginning excavations in the area surrounding the church.

169. Demolition of the modern addition to the church began on April 27, 1954.

"We start to erect the scaffolding for the demolition of the bell tower immediately after Easter recess and finish it at noon, Friday April 30. On Friday afternoon some of the first blocks are removed" (Nb. HA I, p. 142).

170. View of the west end after the bell tower and the roof of the narthex have been removed, May 1954

171. View of the east end of the inner wall of the narthex after plaster has been removed, May 21, 1954. The termination of the north wall of the narthex (left side) shows original Byzantine masonry intact.

172. Interior of the church before the start of the restoration project, March 2, 1954. Before the restoration began the floor was removed and excavations were carried out to determine the church's history.

173. Wooden braces and scaffold erected to support the masonry walls after the removal of the late additions to the narthex

"We resume actual restoration of the church after a visit from Mr. Orlandos, who promises to send a technician to advise on problems of reinforcement and reconstruction" (Nb. HA I, p. 182; May 27, 1954).

174. View of the altar of the church, which was made up of ancient architectural pieces, July 28, 1954

"In excavating in preparation for bracing the arches, we have reached the point where we must remove the Sacred Table. It stands on the axis of the building just outside the mouth of the E apse. The part visible above the latest church floor consists of 4 ancient blocks stacked one on top of the other; from top down: 1) Plinth of Pentelic marble; 2) Doric capital of Pentelic marble; 3) Ionic base of Pentelic marble; 4) Square acanthus capital" (Nb. HA II, pp. 358, 360).

175. The northeast column with scaffold and bracing erected to carry the weight of the vaults in preparation for removing the column, October 7, 1954

176. After the northeast column was removed, a form was inserted and the new concrete column was poured, October 15, 1954.

"We have removed the plaster from all four columns supporting the dome. All except the NE column are monolithic, of gray marble. The SW column is in excellent shape, the only damage being some slight chipping at the bottom. The NW column has been hacked away in the lower part so that little more than half of its original diameter is preserved. The circle was then filled out with later plaster containing much straw. The SE column suffered much, apparently at the time the modern iconostasis was put in place. This is supported by a large iron bar inserted into the sides of the NE and SE columns. This caused the marble to crack vertically from top to bottom in several places.

The NE column [175] is in the worst state of all. It consists of 21 drums of poros, ranging from 0.10 to 0.20 meters high, all out of alignment, resting on one bottom drum of grayish marble 0.40 m. high. Its capital is an Ionic base upside down" (Nb. HA II, pp. 324–326; July 15, 1954).

177. View from the narthex of the eastern apse after excavations. Three of the four columns had been replaced. The southwest column (bottom right) was left in place, January 21, 1955.

81

178. Drawing by John Travlos of the proposed restoration of the vaults of the narthex, 1955

"We have not been entirely satisfied with the proposed system of roofing the narthex, and have re-examined the problem carefully with reference to the existing remains and also to the nearest known parallel, the Palaiopanagia at Manolada, which J.T. [John Travlos] and I visited at New Years. A revised plan was sent to Mr. Orlandos, calling for groin vaults as before, over the innerpilar space flanking the apse, low saucer dome over the NW and SW bays, and a slightly higher saucer dome over the square central area. On February 8, Mr. Orlandos visited the church and approved the new plan" (Nb. HA IV, p. 601a; February 1955).

179. Centering (wooden forms for building the vaults) under construction. View from the southwest, February 21, 1955.

180. Building the centering for the vaults of the central saucer dome and completing the ribbing, February 21, 1955

181. Forms for the vaults of the narthex after laying reinforcing steel and electric conduit for the wiring. View from above, March 22, 1955.

"At 1 p.m. we start pouring the concrete for the roof of the narthex. At 5:45 p.m. we finish the first shape, i.e. to the ring of the saucer domes. This is allowed to set overnight before covering the saucer domes which was done by noon, March 24. The remaining concrete was poured covering all these domes, on March 28, and on March 30 construction of the west apse begins. This is of heavy rubble masonry on the part which will be concealed by the roof of the narthex. The upper part will be of cloisonné" (Nb. HA IV, p. 640; March 23, 1955).

182. The first concrete to be poured for the narthex domes, March 23, 1955

183. Finishing the concrete of the smaller saucer domes of the narthex, March 28, 1955. Work on the central dome is still in progress. The steeper sides and height of the central dome meant that wood forms had to be constructed around the base to hold the concrete in place while pouring.

184. The church from the southwest after completion of the vaulting of the narthex and before beginning final work on the west wall, April 11, 1955. Centering for the western half-dome has been constructed. The windows of the dome have been restored.

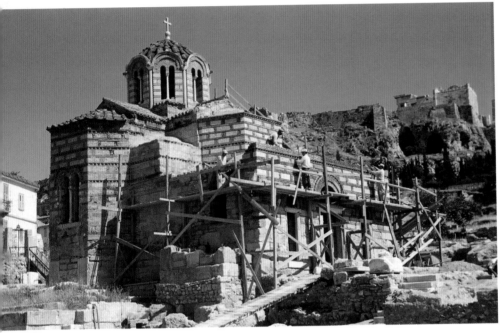

185. The northwest corner of the church, July 6, 1955. The final course of poros masonry has been laid for the west wall and work is progressing on the decorative brick-and-tile crown course.

186. View of the church from the west as the restoration project nears completion, August 1956. The roof tiles of the narthex are being laid.

187 *(above)*. Restoring the masonry of the dome and its windows, spring 1955

The structural elements of the church—the walls, columns, and vaulting—had been restored by late summer of 1955. Still, much work had to be done before the dedication ceremony, planned to coincide with that of the Stoa of Attalos on September 3, 1956. In the coming months, the roof of the narthex was built, the interior walls plastered, the marble floor-paving laid, and the original marble elements of the windows were either restored or modern copies of designs contemporary to the building were set. In addition, the surviving frescoes were conserved, and frescoes that had been removed from the Church of Aghios (Saint) Spyridon and Aghios Georgios were installed in the new narthex.

188 *(above right)*. The unfinished interior of the southern end of the narthex, April 22, 1955. The concrete domes and the walls are still without plaster.

189. Theophanes Nomikos carving the marble lunette for the central doorway, March 8, 1956. The interior walls have been plastered, the southern window of the narthex has been restored, and frescoes have been installed. Compare with 188.

190 *(above)*. View from the narthex into the interior, December 1955. Frescoes from the Church of Aghios Spyridon were reset in the walls of the restored narthex. The fresco of Saint Spyridon was set on the left side of the central door leading into the interior.

191. A watercolor of Saint Spyridon by Piet de Jong, made before the fresco was removed from the chapel of Aghios Spyridon in the 1930s. Piet de Jong, an extraordinary archaeological illustrator, joined the staff of the Agora Excavations in 1932. The two watercolors (**191** and **193**) represent just a tiny fraction of the work he left behind. They also illustrate the remarkable talent he had of coaxing details and colors from the object he was illustrating. His watercolor of the fresco above (**190**) reveals an image of Saint Spyridon with an intensity of color and detail that no longer exists.

192 *(above)*. View from the narthex into the interior, December 1955. The fresco of Saint Anthony, originally in the Church of Aghios Spyridon, was set on the right side of the central door leading into the interior.

193. A watercolor of Saint Anthony by Piet de Jong, made before the fresco was removed from the chapel of Aghios Spyridon. Compare with **192**.

194. The restored dome of the Church of the Holy Apostles with the Pantokrator (The All Powerful) looking down, April 1957. The fresco dates from Period II of the church, and is attributed to the 18th century. It was removed to permit strengthening of the dome and then reinstalled.

195. View of the interior of the church upon completion of the restoration, December 1956

196. View of the northwest corner of the church after restoration, September 1956

197. View of the southeast corner of the church after restoration, September 1956

198. View of the west end of the church after restoration, September 1956

199. Aerial view of the Agora, August 3, 1951. Although more excavations would continue in the Agora (defined by box), the layout of the ancient marketplace was well enough studied by 1953 to permit planning for landscaping the site and designing paths and walkways.

LANDSCAPING

200. Aerial view of the Athenian Agora archaeological park, May 1975. After 20 years of growth, the trees, shrubs, and other plants have reached their maturity. The archaeological remains are clearly visible with paths and walkways to lead the visitor through the park.

LANDSCAPING THE AGORA

As part of the same project to restore the Stoa of Attalos and the Church of the Holy Apostles, the entire arch-aeological site was landscaped and planted in the 1950s in order to turn the excavated area into an archaeological park. A guiding principle was to use plants native to Greece and in particular those known to have been available in antiquity. One instance of ancient planting around the Hephaisteion, recovered by excavation, led to the planting of two rows of bushes—one of pomegranates, the second of myrtle—around the old temple. In all, over 4,500 trees, shrubs, and vines were planted in an effort to render the site more inviting to the visitor, and to provide the city of Athens with much-needed parkland. Paths, benches, and labels for the monuments were also part of the landscaping program.

"*At the same time that the reconstruction was under way on the Stoa of Attalos and the Church of the Holy Apostles, one other commitment was being carried out, the landscaping of the whole excavated area. In August 1953 Ralph E. Griswold, a prominent landscape architect of Pittsburgh, went to Athens to consider the situation, draw up a plan and make an estimate which he submitted in October 1953. An urgent drive for funds from January to June 1954 with the active interest of garden groups in both the United States and Greece proved so encouraging that in June he was authorized to proceed. Work was begun on November 8, 1954, with Ralph Griswold actively supervising the entire operation*" (L. S. Meritt, *History of the American School of Classical Studies at Athens, 1939–1980* [1984], p. 188).

201. View of the Agora from the Acropolis looking northwest, December 1950. The photograph shows the appear-ance of the site when plans for the landscaping project were being made and before the Stoa of Attalos and Church of the Holy Apostles restoration projects had begun.

202. View looking northwest across the Agora before the landscaping project began, from a vantage point near the Church of the Holy Apostles, 1949

203. View looking southeast across the central area of the Agora from the Hephaisteion before the landscape project began, 1949. The circular foundations of the Tholos are visible at the bottom right, the old Excavation House complex can be seen in the middle, and the Stoa of Attalos and Church of the Holy Apostles before restoration to the left.

204. View looking east from the Hephaisteion of the northern portion of the Agora before the landscape project began, 1951. The rectangular area of the Temple of Ares is seen in the foreground, the Odeion and Giants in the middle just to the right, and the unrestored Stoa of Attalos in the background.

The Proposal

" *My visits as a tourist to other excavations enabled me to see how various types of visitors reacted to different ways of treating landscape problems. The results of my observations are incorporated in my recommendations.*

More valuable than almost any other aspect of my study was the opportunity of observing, from the balcony of the office which I shared with Mr. Thompson, the hundreds of visitors who swarmed through the Agora daily. One day I joined the regular Wednesday tours conducted by staff members Perlzweig [Judith Binder] and Eliot [C. W. J. Eliot]. Then I watched similar conducted tours wind their way through the ruins and I checked these routes with Mr. Thompson. By this process the proposed path system which forms the skeleton of the landscape scheme was developed. It is the natural route for visitors to follow and very close to the route followed by Pausanias about the year 150 A.D.

One of the most acute problems for landscape maintenance in Athens is water for irrigation of the plants. Fortunately I was there at the time of the year when this problem was at its worst. The importance of adequate irrigation was very apparent and has been given primary consideration in my recommendations.

Among all the excavations of ancient sites in Greece there is no precedent for the proposed systematic landscape development of the Athenian Agora. This is a pioneer undertaking. It is as unique in modern archaeological practice as the Agora was in its historical significance and will add new interest to its ancient traditions. . . .

The primary purpose of the landscape development is to enhance the historical significance of the ancient Agora. Wherever plants are known to have existed in antiquity the same varieties are to be replanted as near as possible in their original locations. Except for these plants, which are a recorded part of the ancient landscape, the planting has been designed as a background to the structural antiquities.

Likewise, all other elements of the landscape such as fences, walls, walks, steps and benches serve the sole purpose of protecting and providing access to the Agora and its adjacent areas" (Ralph E. Griswold, "Preliminary Report for the Landscape Development," pp. 1–3, dated October 15, 1953).

The Plants

" *The accompanying list of plant materials includes only indigenous plants or plants which have been completely acclimatized. No exotic plants will be used in the historic area except perhaps one palm [tree] on the terrace of the Church of the Holy Apostles.*

Each plant mentioned in historic references or determined definitely by my preliminary study is identified by key number on the preliminary plan. On the other hand, much of the planting has been specified only as to general type leaving the final selection for further detailed study when the working drawings and specifications are prepared. . . .

The large trees, such as the plane and oak which are indicated on the plan with a ten meter foliage spread, will provide convenient shade for visitors and will also frame the important antiquities without obscuring them from various viewpoints. Trees of this size have also been used to screen the view of the railroad.

Smaller trees such as the laurel or carob which are indicated by a three meter foliage spread will also provide shade but will serve primarily as background and markers for the important structures.

Trees with emphatic shapes and dark evergreen foliage such as cypress and pine have been kept out of the central area and used to emphasize the boundaries particularly in the corners and at entrances.

Places where foundations show the former existence of statues to heroes and prominent citizens will be marked by evergreen plants in scale with the foundations. These dark green plants will be seen in the panoramic views much as the statues were seen in antiquity.

On the rocky slopes North and East of the Hephaisteion and North of the Areopagus trees will be planted in the ancient cisterns. These for the most part will be evergreen trees with a few groups of flowering deciduous trees. Between them the rock ledges will be interplanted with native plants such as heather, gorse and thyme which grow naturally in similar habitats.

In the valley between the West boundary and the central area of the Agora moisture-loving trees such as willow and poplar will be planted along the ancient drains.

Around the Hephaisteion the outline of the ancient peribolos will be simulated by a trimmed evergreen buckthorn hedge. Adjacent to this hedge on the South a comparatively flat area devoid of any particular archaeological interest can be transformed into a wild flower garden displaying the beautiful wild flowers for which Attica is famous.

Among the ruins there are several odd corners where wild flowers will be encouraged to grow as ground cover. In general grass surfaces will not be used although there may be a few spots where tropical grasses may be planted. This will be worked out as the planting progresses" (Ralph E. Griswold, "Preliminary Report for the Landscape Development," pp. 9–10, dated October 15, 1953).

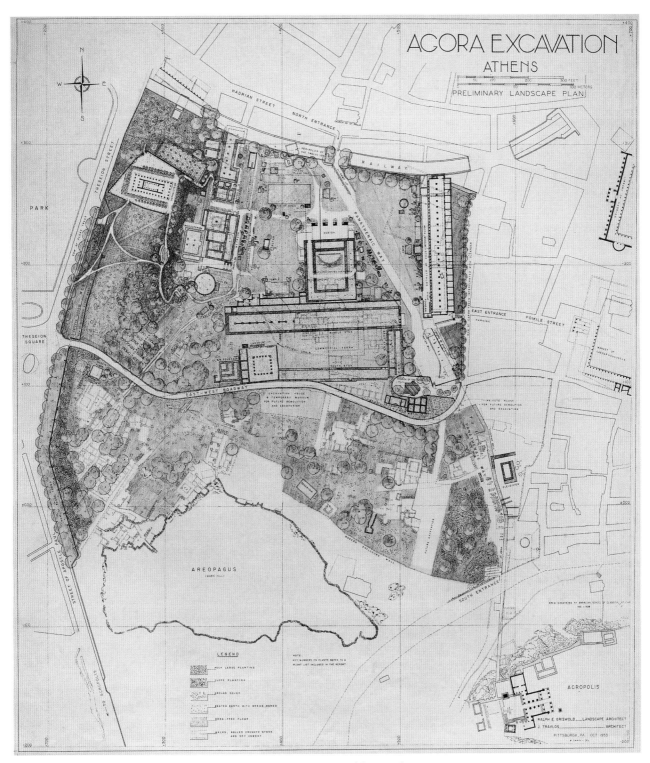

205. Preliminary landscape plan prepared by Ralph E. Griswold, October 1953

A Selection of Trees and Plants Found Today in the Agora

Oriental Plane, *Platanus orientalis*, Πλάτανος

White Poplar, *Populus alba*, Λεύκα

Holm Oak, *Quercus ilex*, Δρύς ή Αριά ή Βαλανιδιά

Judas tree, *Cercis siliquastrum*, Κουτσουπιά

Strawberry tree, *Arbutus unedo*, Κουμαριά

Wild olive tree, *Olea oleaster*, Αγριελιά

Pomegranate, *Punica granatum*, Ροδιά

Almond tree, *Prunus dulcis*, Αμυγδαλιά

Cypress tree, *Cupressus sempervirens*, Κυπαρίσσι

Germander, *Teucrium fruticans*, Τεύκριο

Rosemary, *Rosmarinus officinalis*, Δενδρολίβανο

Myrtle, *Myrtus communis*, Μυρτιά

Oleander, *Nerium oleander*, Ροδοδάφνη

Tree Heather, *Erica arborea*, Ρείκι

Acanthus, *Acanthus mollis*, Ακανθος

Lentisk, *Pistacia lentiscus*, Σχίνος

Mock Orange, *Pittosporum tobira*, Αγγελική

Yellow Jasmine, *Jasminum primulinum*, Γιασεμί κίτρινο

206. View of the central part of the Agora site looking east from the roof of the Hephaisteion, June 1937. Ralph E. Griswold was given four photographs (**206, 209, 212, 215**) of various views of the Agora which showed the general state of the excavations. He took these images and painted on top of them to create an impression of his proposed landscape design.

207. A watercolor painted on top of a photograph (**206**) by Ralph E. Griswold showing his impression of the design for the central part of the Agora site. Note that when he made this painting only a two-thirds reconstruction of the Stoa of Attalos was planned.

208. View of the central part of the Agora site looking east from the Hephaisteion, April 2006

209. View of the central part of the Agora site looking south, July 1950. The Giants of the Odeion are visible in the middle, and behind is the Church of the Holy Apostles before restoration. To the left is the southern portion of the Stoa of Attalos before reconstruction.

210. A watercolor painted on top of a photograph (**209**) by Ralph E. Griswold showing his impression of the design for the central part of the Agora site

211. View of the central part of the Agora site looking south from the rooftop terrace of a building on Hadrian Street, April 2006

97

212. View of the central and western part of the Agora site looking southwest toward the Observatory, October 19, 1951. A terrace retaining wall encloses the area around the Hephaisteion, the large square at the bottom left is the area of the foundations for the Temple of Ares.

213. A watercolor painted on top of a photograph (**212**) by Ralph E. Griswold showing his impression of the landscape design for the central and western part of the Agora site

214. View of the central and western part of the Agora site looking southwest from a vantage point near the north entrance, April 2006. The same view as that of **212**, taken at a greater height, is now impossible to duplicate since the photograph was taken from the roof of a building now removed.

215. View of the southwestern side of the Agora looking northwest toward the hill of Kolonos Agoraios and the Hephaisteion, December 9, 1954. The demolition of the terrace retaining wall began the previous month.

216. A watercolor painted on top of a photograph (215) by Ralph E. Griswold showing his impression of the landscape design for the hill of Kolonos Agoraios and the area surrounding the Hephaisteion

217. View of the hill of Kolonos Agoraios and the area surrounding the Hephaisteion, April 2006

The Garden of Hephaistos

"An unexpected result of the Agora excavations has been the recovery of the setting of the 'Theseion,' now recognized as the temple of Hephaistos. Its beauty can be most fully appreciated from the ancient level of vision—the floor of the market square. Its relation to the life of the Athenians is made vivid by the discovery of the shops of the metalworkers scattered over the hill on which stands the temple of their patron god. And finally, even the vanished temple-close can be restored, the garden of Hephaistos.

This garden survives only in rows of cuttings in the bedrock running parallel to the temple. At first their significance escaped the excavators but when pots appeared in hole after hole, the very duplicates of modern flower pots, only one interpretation was open to even the most incredulous. Yet when we look at the naked rock and gaping holes, it seems almost impossible to replant it, even in imagination" (D. B. Thompson, "The Garden of Hephaistos," Hesperia 6 [1937], p. 396).

218. View of the cuttings in the bedrock of ancient planting holes to the south of the temple, from the roof of the Hephaisteion, June 1936

219. Ancient and modern methods of transplanting. Homer A. Thompson holding a flowerpot used in antiquity for transplanting shrubs in the Hephaisteion garden, and Ralph E. Griswold holding a balled myrtle bush about to be planted, February 11, 1955.

220. View at the southeast corner of the Hephaisteion of the outer myrtle hedge and the inner row of pomegranate bushes planted in 1955 parallel to the temple, April 21, 2006

221. Removing the modern retaining wall in front of the Hephaisteion, November 1954

222. Watercolor of the Hephaisteion, painted by Ralph E. Griswold, showing his impression of the landscape design, 1955

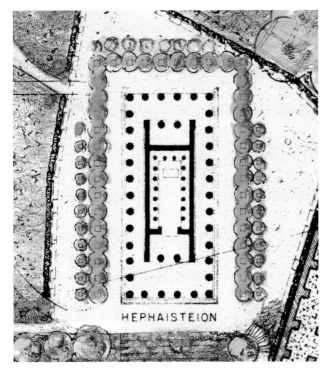

HEPHAISTEION

223 *(above)*. Detail of the preliminary landscape design showing the area surrounding the temple where the modern Garden of Hephaistos was planted

224 *(right)*. View of the Hephaisteion and the path leading up to the temple from a vantage point similar to that of 221, April 21, 2006

PUBLIC AND PRIVATE SUPPORT

The success of the Agora landscape project can be attributed to the remarkable support and cooperation by Greeks and Americans who wished to see the project succeed. Garden societies in Greece and America sent monetary donations; in Greece, private and state nurseries contributed trees, shrubs, vines, and seeds; the Athens Water Company contributed technical expertise to ensure an adequate water supply; and many service organizations volunteered their time to help with the actual planting. The legacy of these individuals is seen today and enjoyed by all visitors to the site.

"This year as last grateful acknowledgement must be made to the many organizations and individuals who have assisted the landscaping program in one way or another. The Athenian Committee for the Landscaping of the Agora has continued its activity by raising money. Attic landowners have again contributed nursery stock. The Boy Scouts and Sea Scouts of Athens and Attica have assisted in the actual planting, while the Athenian Committee and the Association of Autochthonous Athenians have set out symbolic trees. The restoration of the 'Garden of Hephaistos' was made possible by the Garden Club and a number of residents of Princeton, New Jersey, while residents of Providence, Rhode Island have assumed responsibility for the landscaping around the Church of the Holy Apostles. Many individuals have contributed trees, shrubs and benches, often as memorials to friends or relatives.

Thanks are again due to the staff of the Water Company of Athens for much technical assistance in connection with the installation" (H. A. Thompson, "Activities in the Athenian Agora: 1955," *Hesperia* 25 [1956], p. 64).

225:a, b. The project to landscape the Agora was inaugurated on January 4, 1954. King Paul and Queen Frederica each planted trees on either side of the Altar of Zeus Agoraios. In the photograph on the left, the king looks on as his wife, with shovel in hand, helps plant a laurel tree; on the right, smiling broadly, stands Sophokles Lekkas, chief foreman, and just behind is John L. Caskey, director of the American School. The photograph on the right is a view of the now-mature trees, just behind the monument to the Eponymous Heroes, April 21, 2006.

226. Girl Guides of Athens standing in front of the Hephaisteion before setting out to plant laurel trees, December 12, 1954. Note the progress made on demolishing the retaining wall.

"Systematic planting began early in December in the western and northern parts of the Agora. Here too assistance has been received from local groups, notably the Girl Guides of Athens who on December 12th arrived one hundred fifty strong and planted some thirty laurels along the northern edge of the excavation, where they will replace the grove of laurel and of olive that is known to have shaded the ancient Altar of Pity in this area; the new shrubs will at the same time screen from view the retaining wall of the electric railway that skirts the north side of the area" (H. A. Thompson, "Activities in the Athenian Agora: 1954," *Hesperia* 24 [1955], p. 71).

227. Girl Guide planting a laurel tree, December 12, 1954

228. View looking west from below the hill of Kolonos Agoraios toward the Hephaisteion, April 21, 2006

229. A priest blessing an olive tree at a ceremony at the Hephaisteion, February 13, 1955. Ralph E. Griswold and Homer A. Thompson stand in the crowd on the right. The Association of Autochthonous Athenians planted an olive, a fig, and a laurel tree nearby.

230. Boy Scouts and Sea Scouts of Athens and Attica planting oleanders in the area southwest of the temple near the western entrance, February 20, 1955

231. View of the area southwest of the temple near the western entrance, April 21, 2006

232:a, b. In the photo at left, Homer A. Thompson, director of the excavations, and Ward M. Canaday, president of the Trustees of the American School, stand beside a plane tree replanted with funds donated by the Greek community of Toledo, Ohio, August 1, 1955. The tree was planted in the area near the Altar of the Twelve Gods where a statue of Demosthenes was said to have stood and which was shaded by a similar tree. Fifty-one years later (right), the tree has grown considerably and provides ample shade for all who sit beneath its canopy.

233. A group photograph of the landscaping crew on the steps of the Hephaisteion, May 21, 1955. Ralph E. Griswold (sixth from the left of second row) sits with the workmen who helped him transform the Agora excavation into an archaeological park.

234. The landscape crew (Griswold in the center) celebrating their accomplishments, May 21, 1955

235. The Agora Park after 50 years of growth, April 2006. A panoramic view looking east from the Edward Capps Memorial belvedere on Kolonos Agoraios, which provides a splendid overview of the Agora. The Stoa of Attalos (center) marks the eastern border of the Agora, and the Church of the Holy Apostles is just to the south (right).

236:a, b. Many wildflowers were planted throughout the Agora site. Above, a carpet of chamomile (*Matricaria recutita*, Χαμομήλι), and at right, wildflowers near the Tholos, April 21, 2006.

Emmanuel Vathis, a professor of botany at the Agricultural University of Athens worked closely with Ralph E. Griswold in the selection of plants appropriate for the landscaping project. The close collaboration of the two can be appreciated throughout the entire year but especially during springtime when many of the wildflowers and plants chosen by them are in bloom. Professor Vathis continued his association with the Agora Park after Griswold's departure and was called upon to help rejuvenate the Agora Park a number of years later. Vathis, also an accomplished botanical illustrator, selected plants from the Agora as specimens to draw and paint for illustrations which he used teaching his students. A selection of these illustrations was published in his book, *The Plants in the Park of Ancient Agora* (Agricultural University of Athens, 2002).

237. Mallow (*Malva sylvestris*, Μολόχα) blooming in the Agora, April 21, 2006

238. The Agora Excavations staff and workforce, 1933. Archaeologists, staff, foremen, and workmen gathered under the Hephaisteion for a group photograph.

THE STAFF

239. Agora Excavations staff, 1933. Third row (left to right): Charles Spector, Piet de Jong, Arthur Parsons, Eugene Vanderpool, Mary Zelia Pease [Philippides], James Oliver. Second row: Joan Bush [Vanderpool], Elizabeth Dow, Virginia Grace, Gladys Baker, Homer Thompson. Sitting: Lucy Talcott, Benjamin Meritt, Josephine Shear, T. Leslie Shear, Dorothy Burr [Thompson].

240. The staff of the Agora Excavations, 1934. Front row (left to right): Gladys Baker, Joan Bush [Vanderpool], Lucy Talcott, T. Leslie Shear, Josephine Shear, Dorothy Burr [Thompson]. Standing: Sophokles Lekkas, Piet de Jong, Catherine Bunnell, Alison Frantz, Dorothy Traquair, Rodney Young, Eugene Vanderpool, James Oliver, Arthur Parsons, Sterling Dow, Charles Spector, Homer Thompson.

"Professor Shear had numerous qualities which contributed greatly to the School over many years, generosity, vision, vigorous action, but the one for which he will be best remembered and for which the School is most in his debt was his remarkable ability to select a staff of excavation workers of unusual capabilities, to forge them into a harmonious team and to keep them together in their hard-working activities of field work, study and publication, inspired by his own energy and scholarly care for meticulous observation and recording and prompt sharing of results with the scholarly world" (L. S. Meritt, *History of the American School of Classical Studies at Athens, 1939–1980* [1984], p. 176).

241. T. Leslie Shear, director of the Agora Excavations, 1931–1945

242:a, b. Homer A. Thompson, director of the Agora Excavations, 1946–1967

243:a, b. Dorothy Burr Thompson, though diminutive in stature, brought energy and intellectual acumen to her work as an excavator and scholar. At bottom left, she inspects the rock face of the north slope of the Areopagus in 1934; at bottom right, she works on the Agora terracotta figurines. Dorothy married Homer in 1934.

244. Eugene Vanderpool (E.V.) examining a bronze bowl (B 966)

245. E.V. studying the text of the "Law against Tyranny" inscription (I 6524)

246. Affectionately known to students and colleagues by only his initials, Eugene Vanderpool began his career at the Agora in 1932. Later he was appointed Professor of Archaeology of the American School, 1947–1971.

247. E.V. and John Travlos discussing plans for the reconstruction of the Stoa of Attalos, April 1950

248. John Travlos began working at the Agora excavations in 1935.

249. John Travlos, Architect of the School, 1940–1973

250:a, b. At left, Piet de Jong at work in the Old Excavation House, 1937; above, a monogram of the artist.

113

251:a, b. Virginia Grace joined the records staff of the Agora in 1932. Miss Grace is best known for her lifelong study of amphoras from the Agora which she used to form the basis of her research concerning transport amphoras in the Mediterranean.

252:a, b. Lucy Talcott, one the original members of the 1931 staff, was responsible for developing the card catalogue system for the objects. She also coauthored, with Brian Sparkes, *Agora* XII.

253:a, b. Alison Frantz came to the Agora in 1934 as an assistant to Lucy Talcott. An interest in photography was soon rekindled, and by 1939 she was staff photographer of the excavation, a position she held until 1964. Her talent for shooting archaeological subjects was such that she was asked to photograph throughout the Mediterranean, but Frantz was also a Byzantine scholar and she worked closely with John Travlos to restore the Church of the Holy Apostles. She authored two Agora volumes, *Agora* XX and *Agora* XXIV.

254. Margaret Crosby studying architectural fragments in the basement of the Agora museum, 1956. *"Her primary responsibility at the Agora was the supervision of fieldwork, and from 1935 to 1939, and then again from 1946 to 1955, she spent every season in the field"* (Agora Picturebook 26 [2006], p. 53). Crosby also coauthored, with Mabel Lang, *Agora* X, combining her interests in weights and measures and inscriptions.

255:a, b. Rodney Young began excavating in the Agora in 1934. The photographs above were taken in 1947 for an article entitled "Pot's Progress," published in the first issue of *Archaeology* Magazine (vol. 1, no. 1, 1948, p. 13). Young was posed sitting amidst stacks of pottery removed from a well (Deposit A 17:2) that were ready for sorting.

256. James Oliver and his crew of workmen in Section K, 1934. Oliver was an Agora Fellow between 1932 and 1935, excavating in four sections. He also assisted Benjamin Meritt in studying and cataloguing the inscriptions.

257. Group photograph of workmen. The photograph was probably taken in 1933, as a man sitting in the center, identified as the foreman, is the same man sitting at the bottom right of **259**.

116

258. Group photograph taken in front of the Mycenaean chamber tomb found in Section EE, looking south, June 1939. The man standing in the center is likely the excavator of the tomb, Eugene Vanderpool.

259. The foremen at the excavations in 1933. Sophokles Lekkas, the chief foreman, is seated in the middle of the second row with his assistants. Lekkas came to the Agora in 1931 after working many years at the American School's excavations in Corinth.

260. Mary Zelia Pease [Philippides], shown here flanked by Eugene Vanderpool and Virginia Grace, was a member of the staff in 1933. Together with Gladys Baker, she assisted Josephine Shear in cataloguing the coins that year. She returned to the Agora on fellowships in 1957/8 and 1967/8 to study the Attic black-figured pottery, and later coauthored, with Mary B. Moore, *Agora* XXIII. Mrs. Philippides was the Librarian of the School from 1958 to 1971, and is the last surviving member of the excavation's original staff.

SPYROS SPYROPOULOS

The spirit of Spyros Spyropoulos still lingers in the stoa many years after his death. A "jack of all trades," he assisted all who came to the Agora Excavations for research and study. Spyros was the individual behind the scenes who worked tirelessly at any task asked of him. Many fondly remember experiencing a *symposium* hosted by him when he relaxed, often in the nearby Epirus Taverna.

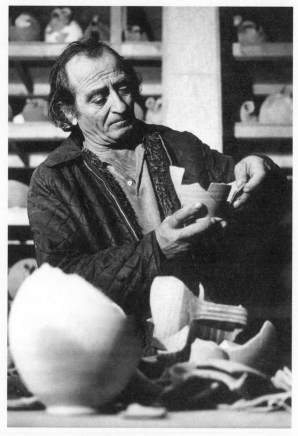

261:a, b. Spyros Spyropoulos making a cast of a Dacian (S 2518) *(above left)* and mending a pot *(above)*

262 *(left)*. Caretaker of an injured owl that had found shelter in the Agora, Spyros and Bouphos contemplate each other in the upper colonnade.

263. A *symposium* held by Spyros at the Epirus Taverna, July 1975: (left to right) John Traill, Hardy Hansen, Spyros, the waiter, Dan Geagan, and Merle Langdon.

"A Radical Departure in the Conduct of Excavation"

In 1980, there was a major change in the way the Agora was excavated. While a professional staff was maintained, including a core group of experienced Greek workmen, the actual digging would be done for the first time by student volunteers. A complete list of these volunteers may be found at the end of this volume.

264. The staff of 1980 and visiting scholars. Standing (left to right): Leslie Mechem, Spyros Spyropoulos, Sally Roberts, Susan Rotroff, Robert Pounder, Lynn Grant, Helen Townsend, Mary Moore, Malcolm Wallace, Steve Koob, Alison Adams, Margie Miles, Robert Vincent, Kyriaki Moustaki. Sitting: John Camp, T. Leslie Shear Jr., Dorothy Thompson, Homer Thompson, Virginia Grace, Bill Dinsmoor Jr.

265. Excavation staff, 1980. From left to right: Kostas Pikoulas and his father, Elias Pikoulas, foreman Nikos Dervos, Yiannis Dedes, Ioannis Paipetis, Dionysios Soundias.

Scholarship and Education

One of the great benefits of the Agora Excavations has been its effect on publication and education in classical studies in the United States. In all, over 150 scholars have contributed books or articles on the results of the excavations, while since 1980 more than 470 students, representing over 100 colleges and universities, have excavated on the site. The following pages record this widespread participation.

Agora Bibliography

THE ATHENIAN AGORA SERIES

I: *Portrait Sculpture,* E. B. Harrison, 1953
II: *Coins from the Roman through the Venetian Period,* M. Thompson, 1954
III: *Literary and Epigraphical Testimonia,* R. E. Wycherley, 1957
IV: *Greek Lamps and Their Survivals,* R. H. Howland, 1958
V: *Pottery of the Roman Period: Chronology,* H. S. Robinson, 1959
VI: *Terracottas and Plastic Lamps of the Roman Period,* C. Grandjouan, 1961
VII: *Lamps of the Roman Period: First to Seventh Century after Christ,* J. Perlzweig, 1961
VIII: *Late Geometric and Protoattic Pottery: Mid 8th to Late 7th Century B.C.,* E. T. H. Brann, 1962
IX: *Islamic Coins,* G. C. Miles, 1962
X: *Weights, Measures, and Tokens,* M. Lang and M. Crosby, 1964
XI: *Archaic and Archaistic Sculpture,* E. B. Harrison, 1965
XII: *Black and Plain Pottery of the 6th, 5th, and 4th Centuries B.C.,* B. A. Sparkes and L. Talcott, 1970
XIII: *The Neolithic and Bronze Ages,* S. A. Immerwahr, 1971
XIV: *The Agora of Athens: The History, Shape, and Uses of an Ancient City,* H. A. Thompson and R. E. Wycherley, 1972
XV: *Inscriptions: The Athenian Councillors,* B. D. Meritt and J. S. Traill, 1974
XVI: *Inscriptions: The Decrees,* A. G. Woodhead, 1997
XVII: *Inscriptions: The Funerary Monuments,* D. W. Bradeen, 1974
XVIII: *Inscriptions: The Dedications,* D. Geagan (forthcoming)
XIX: *Inscriptions: Horoi, Poletai Records, and Leases of Public Lands,* G. V. Lalonde, M. K. Langdon, M. B. Walbank, 1991
XX: *The Church of the Holy Apostles,* A. Frantz, 1971
XXI: *Graffiti and Dipinti,* M. L. Lang, 1976
XXII: *Hellenistic Pottery: Athenian and Imported Moldmade Bowls,* S. I. Rotroff, 1982
XXIII: *Attic Black-Figured Pottery,* M. B. Moore and M. Z. P. Philippides, 1986
XXIV: *Late Antiquity: A.D. 267–700,* A. Frantz, 1988
XXV: *Ostraka,* M. Lang, 1990
XXVI: *The Greek Coins,* J. H. Kroll with A. S. Walker, 1993
XXVII: *The East Side of the Agora,* R. F. Townsend, 1995
XXVIII: *The Lawcourts at Athens,* A. L. Boegehold et al., 1995
XXIX: *Hellenistic Pottery: Athenian and Imported Wheelmade Table Ware and Related Material,* S. I. Rotroff, 1997
XXX: *Attic Red-Figured and White-Ground Pottery,* M. B. Moore, 1997
XXXI: *The City Eleusinion,* M. M. Miles, 1998

HESPERIA SUPPLEMENTS

No. 1: *Prytaneis: A Study of the Inscriptions Honoring the Athenian Councillors,* S. Dow, 1937
No. 2: *Late Geometric Graves and a Seventh-Century Well in the Agora,* R. S. Young, 1939
No. 4: *The Tholos of Athens and Its Predecessors,* H. A. Thompson, 1940
No. 5: *Observations on the Hephaisteion,* W. B. Dinsmoor, 1941
No. 8: *Commemorative Studies in Honor of Theodore Leslie Shear,* 1949
No. 9: *Horoi: Studies in Mortgage, Real Security, and Land Tenure in Ancient Athens,* J. V. A. Fine, 1951
No. 12: *The Athenian Constitution after Sulla,* D. J. Geagan, 1967
No. 13: *Marcus Aurelius: Aspects of Civic and Cultural Policy in the East,* J. H. Oliver, 1970

No. 14: *The Political Organization of Attica*, J. S. Traill, 1975

No. 17: *Kallias of Sphettos and the Revolt of Athens in 286 B.C.*, T. L. Shear Jr., 1978

No. 19: *Studies in Attic Epigraphy, History, and Topography Presented to Eugene Vanderpool*, 1982

No. 20: *Studies in Athenian Architecture, Sculpture, and Topography Presented to Homer A. Thompson*, 1982

No. 22: *Attic Grave Reliefs That Represent Women in the Dress of Isis*, E. J. Walters, 1988

No. 23: *Hellenistic Relief Molds from the Athenian Agora*, C. Grandjouan, 1989

No. 25: *Debris from a Public Dining Place in the Athenian Agora*, S. I. Rotroff and J. H. Oakley, 1992

No. 29: *The Athenian Grain-Tax Law of 374/3 B.C.*, R. S. Stroud, 1998

No. 31: *Ceramicus Redivivus: The Early Iron Age Potters' Field in the Area of the Classical Athenian Agora*, J. K. Papadopoulos, 2003

AGORA PICTURE BOOKS

1: *Pots and Pans of Classical Athens*, B. A. Sparkes and L. Talcott, 1959

2: *The Stoa of Attalos II in Athens*, H. A. Thompson, 1959 (rev. 1992)

3: *Miniature Sculpture from the Athenian Agora*, D. B. Thompson, 1959

4: *The Athenian Citizen*, M. Lang, 1960 (rev. 2004, J. Camp)

5. *Ancient Portraits from the Athenian Agora*, E. B. Harrison, 1960

6. *Amphoras and the Ancient Wine Trade*, V. R. Grace, 1961 (rev. 1979)

7. *The Middle Ages in the Athenian Agora*, A. Frantz, 1961

8. *Garden Lore of Ancient Athens*, R. E. Griswold and D. B. Thompson, 1963

9. *Lamps from the Athenian Agora*, J. Perlzweig, 1963

10. *Inscriptions from the Athenian Agora*, B. D. Meritt, 1966

11. *Waterworks in the Athenian Agora*, M. Lang, 1968

12. *An Ancient Shopping Center: The Athenian Agora*, D. B. Thompson, 1971 (rev. 1993)

13. *Early Burials from the Agora Cemeteries*, S. A. Immerwahr, 1973

14. *Graffiti in the Athenian Agora*, M. Lang, 1974 (rev. 1988)

15. *Greek and Roman Coins in the Athenian Agora*, F. S. Kleiner, 1975

16. *The Athenian Agora: A Short Guide*, J. Camp, 2003; Greek edition 2004

17. *Socrates in the Agora*, M. Lang, 1978

18. *Mediaeval and Modern Coins in the Athenian Agora*, F. S. Kleiner, 1978

19. *Gods and Heroes in the Athenian Agora*, J. Camp, 1980

20. *Bronzeworkers in the Athenian Agora*, C. C. Mattusch, 1982

21. *Ancient Athenian Building Methods*, J. Camp and W. B. Dinsmoor Jr., 1984

22. *Birds of the Athenian Agora*, R. D. Lamberton and S. I. Rotroff, 1985

23. *Life, Death, and Litigation in the Athenian Agora*, M. Lang, 1994

24. *Horses and Horsemanship in the Athenian Agora*, J. Camp, 1998

25. *The Games at Athens*, J. Neils and S. V. Tracy, 2003

26. *Women in the Athenian Agora*, S. I. Rotroff and R. D. Lamberton, 2006

27. *Marbleworkers in the Athenian Agora*, C. Lawton, 2006

GUIDES AND MISCELLANEOUS VOLUMES

The Athenian Agora: A Guide to the Excavations, 1954 (1st edition, M. Lang and C. W. J. Eliot)

The Athenian Agora: A Guide to the Excavations, 1962 (2nd edition, H. A. Thompson)

The Athenian Agora: A Guide to the Excavation and Museum, 1976 (3rd edition, H. A. Thompson)

The Athenian Agora: A Guide to the Excavation and Museum, 1990 (4th edition, J. Camp)

The Athenian Agora: Excavations in the Heart of Classical Athens, J. Camp, London 1986, 1992; Greek edition 2005

The Birth of Democracy (Exhibition Catalogue), J. Camp and D. Buitron-Oliver, 1993; Greek edition 1993

ARTICLES

HESPERIA, the Journal of the ASCSA, was started in 1932, in large part in order to publish the results of the work in the Agora: *"Particularly, the excavations of the Ancient Agora of Athens, which the School commenced in 1931, will find in Hesperia their first full presentation, beginning with this journal's next number"* (Rhys Carpenter, 1932). Since then, some 400 articles on Agora material have appeared in its pages.

STAFF OF THE AGORA EXCAVATIONS, 1931–2006

Karen Abend
Anastasios Adossides
Mark Alonge
Amandina Anastassiades
Richard Anderson
Lawrence Angel
Gladys Baker
Yiannis Bakirzis
Joannes Bakoules
Helen Besi
Judith Perlzweig Binder
Alan Boegehold
Eva Brann
Edwin Brown
Anne Brysbaert
Catherine Bunnell
Earl Caley
Abby Camp
John McK. Camp II
Margot Camp
Janet Carnochan
Elizabeth Caskey
Sarah Caspi
Claudia Chemello
Margaret Cornelius
Margaret Crosby
Constance Curry
Thomas Czarnowski
Kevin Daly
Piet de Jong
George Delleas
Poly Pamel Demoulini
Andreas Demoulinis
Giorgos Dervos
Nikos Dervos
Alison Adams Dickey
William B. Dinsmoor Jr.
Michael Djordjevitch
Norman Doenges
Elizabeth Dow
Sylvie Dumont
Colin Edmonson
G. Roger Edwards
Charles Edwards
Charles Eliot
Freya Evenson
Marie Farnsworth
Patricia Felch
Ruth Fiesel
Alison Frantz
Laura Gawlinski
Virginia Grace
James Graham
Claireve Grandjouan
Aliki Halepa-Bikaki
Katherine Hall
Suzanne Halstead
Marcie Handler
Evelyn Harrison

Bruce Hartzler
Elizabeth Hendrix
James Heyle
Giulia Hitsanides
Marian Holland
Ross Holloway
Anne Hooton
Richard Howland
Emiliya Ivanova
Evan Jenkins
Marian Jenkins
Martin Jones
Jan Jordan
Georgia Karagianni-Giorgoulea
Catherine Keesling
Fred Kleiner
Caroline Koehler
Ellen Kohler
Aziza Kokoni
Maria Komi
Stephen Koob
K. Korizes
John Kroll
Lucy Weier Krystallis
Pia Kvarnström
Gerald Lalonde
Mabel Lang
Michael Laughy
Sophokles Lekkas
Fred Ley
Karen Lovén
Mark Mancuso
Irini Marathaki
Samantha Martin
Craig Mauzy
Marie Mauzy
Eleni Mavriki
Anne McCabe
Benjamin Meritt
Thomas Milbank
Margaret Miles
Marion Miles
Stella Grobel Miller
Stephen Miller
Charles Morgan II
Kyriaki Moustaki
George Nikolaides
Zacharias Nikolaou
John Oates
James Oliver
Nomiki Palaiokrassa
Lena Papachristodoulou
Charikleia Papadopoulou
Arthur Parsons
Alice Boccia Paterakis
Christopher Pfaff
Barbara Philippaki
Mary Pease Philippides
Clare Pickersgill

Wendy Porter
Doris Raymond
Ellen Reeder
Lee Ann Riccardi
Henry Robinson
Susan Rotroff
James Rubright
Effie Sakellaraki
Maria Savvatianou-Petropoulakou
David Scahill
Geoffrey Schmalz
Eugene Schweigert
Louise Capps Scranton
Ione M. Shear
Josephine Platner Shear
Julia Shear
T. Leslie Shear
T. Leslie Shear Jr.
James Sickinger
Angelique Sideris
Mary Wyckoff Simpkin
Grigoris Siolos
Weak Gardner Smith
Evelyn Smithson
Vassilis Spanos
Charles Spector
Spyros Spyropoulos
Maria Stamatatou
Karen Stamm
Richard Stillwell
Gerald Sullivan
Lucy Talcott
Olympia Theofanopoulou
Carol Thomas
Dorothy Burr Thompson
Homer A. Thompson
Margaret Thompson
Margaret Thomson
Emily Townsend
Helen Townsend
Dorothy Traquair
John Travlos
Julie Unruh
Eugene Vanderpool
Eugene Vanderpool Jr.
Joan Bush Vanderpool
Nikos Vasilopoulos
Robert Vincent Jr.
Frederick Waagé
Hermann Wagner
Alan Walker
David Walton
Elisabeth Washburn
Marian Welker
Clayton Whipple
Rebecca Wood
Rodney Young
Ismene Zavitzianou

266. Agora staff and student volunteers, 1980. Front row (left to right): Martha Payne, Vasso Petsas, Kathi Donahue, Liz Bartman, Frayna Goodman, Jody Melander, Athena Sax, Chris Renaud, Nadine McGann, Alexandra Shear, Betsy Flood. Second row: Marc Pershan, Lora Johnson, Panetha Nychis, Lisa DeRensis, Judy Weinstein, Mary Lou Ross, Ann Bozorth, Julia Shear, Pam Posey, Bonnie Leah Griffin, Ann Schelpert, Barbara Hamann, Nancy Moore. Third row: Georgia Karagianni-Giorgoulea, Brian McConnell, Dean Politis, Claire Gabriel, Margie Miles, Alison Adams, Helen Townsend, Ione Shear, Peter Zimmerman, Pam Coravos, Charles Hedrick, Kyriaki Moustaki. Fourth row: Andy Sherwood, Frank DeMita, Richard Liebhart, Hans vander Leest, John Camp, Leslie Shear, Bill Dinsmoor, Richard Hamblen, Kevin Donovan, Mark Fullerton, Robert Vincent.

STUDENT VOLUNTEERS, 1980–2005

Alison Adams (1980)
Brandi Adams (1998)
Elizabeth Afentaki (2002)
Aileen Ajootian (1989)
Austin Akey (2004)
Susan Alcock (1982)
Danielle Allen (1993)
Joel Allen (1994)
L. Allen [1989/93]
Mark Alonge (1995–2000)
Jena Altherr (2003, 2004)
Matthew Amatruda (1991–1993)
Demi Andrianou (1995)
Carla Antonaccio (1982)
Ricardo Apostol (2005)
Iain Arthy (1981)
James Artz (2005)

Sidney Babcock (1982)
Mark Balding (1982)
Adam Barcan (1998)
Laura Barnett (1981)
Bethann Barresi (1999)
Jeremy Bartczak (2001)
Elizabeth Bartman (1980)

Matthew Baumann (2003–2005)
Virginia Baydoun (2001)
Susan Bear (1982)
Margaret Beck (1980)
Robert Behrendt (1990)
Kristen Bellamy (2005)
D. Benetz [1989/93]
Rikke Berg (2005)
Melanie Bernstein (1992)
Julia Billingsley (1981)
Erin Black (1997)
Paul Blomerus (2001)
Dylan Bloy (1994)
Annmarie Bobak (2004, 2005)
Garry Bohm (1980)
Victoria Bok (1981)
Brent Bonds (2002–2005)
Ashley Bones (2005)
Leanna Boychenko (2002)
Joanne Boyer (1994)
Ann Bozorth (1980)
Jorge Bravo (1989–1991)
Thea Brennan-Krohn (2002, 2003)
Christian Brenner (1989, 1990)
Mely Brittingham (1997)

Kathleen Brody (1998)
Deborah Brown (1995)
Jennifer Brown (1999, 2000)
Lori Ann Brown (1993)
Ari Bryen (2004)
Ian Bunker (1997)
Stephen Buonopane (1990)
Kim Burgess (1989)

Elizabeth Calvelo (1991–1993)
Anna Camp (2003)
Fotini Canonis (1998, 1999)
Elizabeth Cantile (2005)
Christina Chong (2002, 2003)
Kimberley Christensen (1998)
Morgan Clendaniel (2004)
Eric Cline (1982)
Anthony Collatos (1992)
Katherine Collins (1989–1991)
Molly Connors (2003)
Pamela Coravos (1980)
Ioanna Coucounis (1993, 1994)
Ted Coulson (1989)
Kerri Cox (1989–1991)
Sandy Crispin (1997)

Eric Csapo (1982)
Christine Cummings (1990)
David Cunningham (1990)
Colette Czapski (1990, 1991)

Kevin Daly (1995)
Emily Davis (2003)
Erin Davis (2000–2002)
John Davis (1990)
Amy Day (1996)
Michael Decker (2001–2005)
Amber DeLuca (2002–2005)
Frank DeMita (1980)
Christi Dennis (1990, 1991)
Lisa DeRensis (1980)
Andrea Diaz (1989)
Joseph DiLuzio (2003, 2004)
Michael Djordjevitch (1990–1994, 1999)
Keith Doherty (2002)
Ben Dolinka (1993, 1994)
Karen Donahue (1998)
Kathleen Donahue (1980)
Kevin Donovan (1980)
J. Downs [1992/93]
Wendy Dowse (1996)
Christina Dufner (1982)
Carrie Duncan (1999)
Warren Dunn (2003)

Melissa Eaby (1998–2000)
Jason Earle (2003, 2004)
Cynthia Eberly (1982)
Katherine (Kitty) Eldred (1992)
Eleni Eliades (1998)
Sigrid Eliassen (2002–2005)
Denise Ellestad (1982)
Lisa Ellis (2000)
Brice Erickson (1992)

Erin Fairburn (2003, 2004)
Elizabeth (Lisa) Farlie (1981)
Anne Feltovich (2003)
Anne Fergman (1981)
Sarah Ferrario (1997)
Ryan Fetters (1997–1999)
Molly Field (2002, 2004)
Elizabeth Flood (1980)
Steven Foy (1995, 1996)
Rachel Friedman (1989)
Mark Fullerton (1980)

Claire Gabriel (1980)
Shrita Gajendragadkar (1997, 1998, 2000)
William Gallaher (1992)
Meghan Gandy (2003–2005)
Alex Gantos (1992–1994)
Joseph Garnjobst (1989–1993)
Laura Gawlinski (1995)
Carolyn Giannopoulos (1998–2001)

Jessica Gingras (2005)
Justin Glanville (1996)
Peter Goldstein (1982)
Frayna Goodman (1980)
Marie Goodwin (1982)
Jody Gordon (2001, 2002)
Sarah Graff (1990)
Vanessa Grahn (1993)
Carlyn Grainger (2001)
Lynn Grant (1981)
Vaughn Greene (1989)
James Gregory (2000)
Charles Griebel (1990, 1991)
Bonnie Leah Griffin (1980)
Cynthia Griffin (1982)
Candis Griggs (1998)
Matthew Grimes (1991)
Richard Grossmann (2005)
Melanie Grunow (1993)
Joann Gulizio (2000–2003)
Victoria Gyori (2002)

Antonius Haakman (1991)
Donald Haggis (1982)
Charles Hailey (1991)
Barbara Hamann (1980)
Richard Hamblen (1980)
Soren Handberg (2002)
Marcie Handler (1997)
John Hansen (1996)
Katherine Harrington (2005)
Matthew Harrington (1999–2002)
Colin Havers (1981, 1982)
Christopher Hawks (2004)
Melissa Hawks (2004)
Marina Haworth (2002, 2003)
Brittany Hayden (2005)
Charles Hedrick (1980)
Sean Hemingway (1989, 1990)
Chad Henneberry (1994, 1996)
Cecilia Hernandez (1999)
Amanda Herring (2001)
Alec Hicks (2004)
Tracie Hill (1992, 1993)
Jeanne Hines (1995)
Stephen Hoban (1998, 1999)
Johanna Hobratschk (2004, 2005)
Melanie Hobson (1991)
Michael Hoff (1981, 1982)
Alan Hogg (1993)
Emily Holt (2001)
Marjorie Horne (1989)
Lizabeth Houchin (1994)
Carla Houle (1989, 1990)
Timothy Howe (1995)
Emily Hughes (1999, 2000)
Robert Huitt (1996, 1997)
Elisabeth Hulette (2004)
Karen Hutchinson (1981)

Juana Ibanez (1981)
Leslie Ike (1981)
Sergey Ilyaschenko (1997, 1998)

Elizabeth Janis (1997)
Patrick Jennett (2004)
Justin Jennings (1994)
Ake Johansson (1994)
Cushman Johnson (2002, 2003)
Jeremy Johnson (1998–2000)
Lora Lee Johnson (1980)
Robert Johnston (1993)
Amy Jones (1995)
Janet Jones (1981)
Emily Jusino (2001)

Amalia Kakissis (1997, 1998)
Alex Kalangis (1989)
Dana Kalleres (1994)
Mark Kampert (2004)
Tanya Kane (1997–1999)
Steve Kangas (1989)
Suzanne Kauffman (1989, 1990)
Catherine Keesling (1993)
Kara Kelly (1990)
Anne Kenner (1982)
Henry Kim (1992)
Jennifer Kimberlin (1992)
Christopher King (1982)
Thomas Klassen (1990, 1991)
Ann-Marie Knoblauch (1995)
Lorraine Knop (2002)
Tallulah Knopp (2005)
Jennifer Knox (2000, 2001)
Jennifer Kochman (1989)
Jessica Koepfler (2003)
Margaret Kondash (1997)
Michael Kowalczuk (1980)
Constantinos Kralios (1991)
Rebecca Krawiec (1990)
Naomi Kroll (1992)
Thomas Kuhn (1998)

Laetitia LaFollette (1981)
Jessica Langenbucher (1998, 1999)
Adriaan Lanni (1995)
Scott Larson (1991)
Michael Laughy (1995)
Sellars Lawrence (1992–1994)
Gregory Leftwich (1981, 1982)
Robert Legander (2002)
Paul Legutko (1993, 1994)
Alexandra Lesk (1994, 1995)
Rachel Levine (1997, 1999)
Emily Lewis (1992)
Joshua Lewis (1996)
Thomas Lide (2001–2003)
Richard Liebhart (1980, 1981)
Joey Lillywhite (1999–2003)
Ian Limbach (1993, 1994)

Michael Lindblom (1994)
Gabriella Lini (2005)
Lisa Little (1991, 1992)
Alexandra Logotheti (1992, 1993)
Ariane Lourie (1991)
Kelly Low (1993, 1994)
Susan Lupack (1996, 1997)
Jennifer Lynn (1989)
Lori Lytle (1993–1995)

William MacCary (1982)
Camilla MacKay (1991)
Riley Maginnis (1981)
Jodi Magness (1982)
Joanna Malandrenias (2004, 2005)
Marc Mancuso (1990, 1991)
Alyssa Mandel (2000)
John Maniatis (1998, 1999)
David Marshall (2000)
Jennifer Martin (1997)
Samantha Martin (2000)
Susan Martin (2002)
Brooke Masek (2005)
David Massey (2004)
Eleni Mavriki (2002, 2003)
Kenneth Mayer (1993)
Anne McCabe (1996)
Matthew McCallum (2001–2005)
Molly McColgan (1991, 1992)
Brian McConnell (1980)
Andrew McCune (1991)
Nadine McGann (1980)
Elizabeth McGowan (1981)
Michael McGrann (1995)
Molly McGraw (1981)
Minnie McMahon (2005)
Joan (Jody) Melander (1980–1982)
Deanna Mellican (2000, 2001)
Benjamin Millis (1999)
Charles Mercier (1989, 1991)
Elizabeth Meyer (1981, 1982)
Hilary Meyrick (1989, 1992)
Andreya Michaloew (1998–2000)
Alison Mickens (1982)
Maria Mikedakis (2000, 2001)
Thomas Milbank (1990, 1991)
Benjamin Milligan (1993)
Nancy Moore (1980)
Corinne Moran (1994, 1995)
Abigail Mulligan (1994)
David Murray (2000, 2001)
Lawrence Myer (2002, 2003)
Teresa Myers (2000)

Anthea Nardi (2002)
E. Nason [1992/93]
Eric Nemeth (1992)
Melpomene Nikiphoridou (1999, 2000)
Jennifer Nilson (2001)
Mia Noerenberg (1991)

Kirk Norman (2002, 2003, 2005)
Anaka Nunnink (2000, 2001, 2003, 2004)
Panetha Nychis (1980)

Thomas Oakley (2000)
Claudia Ocello (1989)
Kanela Oikonomaki (2004)
Emily Oken (1990)
Lada Onyshkevych (1989)
Cynthia Orr (1980)
Adrian Ossi (1999, 2000)
Jeremy Ott (2005)
Elvis Oxley (1994)
Cigdem Ozbek (1997)

Catherine Pack (1996)
Holly Packard (2004)
Jessica Paga (2005)
Amanda Palik (1997)
Aaron Palmore (2005)
George Panos (2002)
Chryssanthi Papadopoulou (2004)
Catherine Parker (1996)
Katherine Parker (1995)
Richard Parker (1981)
Martha Payne (1980–1982)
Barbara Pearce (1993, 1994)
Benjamin Pearlman (1993)
Alina Pellicer (1993)
Marc Pershan (1980, 1981)
Maria Perstedt (1981, 1982)
Erika Peterson (1989, 1990)
Vassoula Petsas (1980)
Claes Pettersson (1981)
Seth Pevnick (1999, 2001, 2003)
Richard Pianka (1990)
Stephen Pigman (1993)
Iris Plaitakis (1995, 1996)
Kevin Pluta (1999–2003)
Constantine Politis (1980, 1981)
Rachel Popelka (1996)
Dominic Popielski (1996)
Jennifer Poppel (2003–2005)
Pamela Posey (1980, 1981)
John Prodromidis (1994)
Jessica Pryde (2001)
Jeffrey Purinton (1982)

Travis Quay (1997, 1998)

Tanya Rabourn (1991–1993)
Alan Rawn (1981)
Andrea Redford (1996, 1997)
Michael Rehberg (1994)
Kaari Reierson (1989)
Pontus Reimers (1981)
Thomas Reinhart (1990, 1991)
Amanda Reiterman (2004, 2005)
Jane Rempel (1994)

Christine Renaud (1980–1982)
Lee Ann Riccardi (1992)
Brandy Robertson (1997)
Thomas Roby (1980)
Bonnie Rock (2001)
Guy Rogers (1982)
Karen Ros (1981)
Heather Rosmarin (1992, 1993)
Mary Louise Ross (1980–1982)
Marcela Rossello (1999)
Elizabeth Rossi (1993)
Anne Ruckdeschel (1991)
Nicholas Rummell (2004)
Terence Rusnak (1990, 1993)
Joel Rygorsky (2000–2003)

Jennifer Sacher (2000, 2001)
Daniel Sahlen (2005)
Ewa Samuelsson (1981, 1982)
Juliana Sander (1996)
Stephen Sarles (1997)
Athena Sax (1980–1982)
Karen Saylor (1994)
David Scahill (1994 ff.)
Benjamin Schalit (1981)
Kathleen Schamel (1982)
Ann Schelpert (1980)
Robert Schon (1992)
Ned Schoolman (2000)
Chad Schroeder (2003)
Matthew Schrumpf (2000, 2001)
Susan Schumacher (2001)
Lisa Schwartz (1981)
Kristin Seaman (1993–1995)
Phoebe Segal (1999, 2000)
Nancy Serwint (1981, 1982)
Julia Shear (1989)
Andrew Sherwood (1980)
Thomas Silverman (1996, 1997)
Brooke Simpson (2001)
David Skoog (1989, 1991)
J. Michael Smiles (1982)
Amy Smith (1996)
Angus Smith (1990)
Christine Smith (2000–2002)
Dawn Smith (1996, 1997)
Karen Smith (1982)
Michael Smith (1996)
Caroline Smitter (1982)
Annabel Snowden (1994)
Susannah Snowden (1994)
Amy Spagna (1995)
Beth Ann Spyrison (1990, 1991)
Jill Stauffer (1990)
Heidi Steinmetz (1991, 1992)
Chad Sterbenz (2000, 2001)
Karen Stern (1998)
Doyle Stevick (1995)
Shari Stocker (1981)
Laura Surtees (2003)

Natalie Taback (1996)
Martha Taylor (1982)
Suzanne Tetrault (2000)
Elizabeth Theran (1993)
Megan Thomsen (2005)
Robert Thurlow (1990)
Kathryn Tiffany (2004)
Marcus Toconita (2001)
Alison Trimpi (1982)
Kenneth Tuite (1997)

Gretchen Umholtz (1981, 1982)

Alexander Vacek (2004)
Floris van den Eijnde (1997)
Johannes vander Leest (1980–1982)
Jeffrey Vanderpool (1995, 1996)
Hettie Veneziano (1994, 1995)

William Wagner (1981)
Sarah Wahlberg (1999)

John Wallrodt (1995)
Alexander Walthall (2004, 2005)
Mark Walton (1998)
Corrie Ward (1998)
Jake Watson (1993)
Margaret Watters (1992)
Judith Weinstein (1980)
Mary Grace Weir (1992)
Robert Weir (1992)
Aviva Weiss (1982)
Martin Wells (2002, 2003)
Jason Wetta (1994)
Polly Wheaton (1982)
Christopher White (1997–1999)
Jerard White (2002)
Andrew Wilburn (1996)
Geoffrey Wilcox (1981, 1982)
Henrietta Wiley (1989, 1990)
Jaime Wilson (1994, 1995)
Paul Wilson (1999)
Sian Wiltshire (1992)

Susan Wise (1993–1995)
Christopher Witmore (1995)
Cynthia Wood (1997, 1998)
Heather Wood (1989)
Aaron Woolf (1981, 1982)
Brandon Worrell (1991–1993, 1996, 1997)
Bonnie Wright (2005)
Charles Wyrick (1992)

Dany Yezbick (1999)
Christopher Young (2003–2005)

Maria Zachariou (2003, 2004)
Melanie Zahab (1994, 1995)
Elizabeth Zegos (2005)
Claire Zimmerman (1981)
Peter Zimmerman (1980)
Christine Zitrides (1993–1995)

Conservation Interns and Volunteers

Amandina Anastassiades (1996)
Koula Asiatidou (1996)
Ioannis Balis (1995)
Gwynne Barney (2001)
Barresi Bethann (1999)
Victoria Brown (2005)
Kim Cullen Cobb (2005)
Tania Collas (1994)
Tina de Domingo (1996)
Elizabeth Demoulas (1988)
Lisa Ellis (2002)
Marilia Fotopoulou (2004)
Candis Griggs (1998)
Hope Gumprecht (1992)
Emily Holt (2001)
Anita Horn (2001)
Audrey Jawando (1999)
Daniel Jöst (2001)
Johanna Kangas (1998)
Vicky Karas (2004)

Hiroko Kariya (1994)
Lisa Kelman (1997)
Jennifer Knox (1999)
M. Larentzakis (1986)
Laura Lipcsei (1999)
Karen Lovén (2004)
Bianca Madden (2000)
A. Moraitou (1992)
Ioanna Moriatou (1995)
Teresa Myers (2000)
Sarah Nunberg (1995)
Krzysztof Olszowski (2004)
Susanna Pancaldo (1995)
Aleksandra Papis (2004)
Smaragda Patsavoura (1990)
Anthea Phoca (2004)
Sari Pouta (1998)
Lisa Pryke (1992)
Paulette Reading (2003)
Marcela Rossello (1999)

Malaika Scheer (2003)
Maria Sek (2004)
Batyah Shtrum (2003)
Martha Singer (1996)
Melina Smirniou (2005)
Brenda Smith (1995)
Helen Stergiadis (1997)
Liz Tipton (2001)
Catherine Triandafyllou (1989)
Konstantina Tsatsouli (2002)
Maria Tziotziou (1997)
Lieve Vandenbulcke (1985)
Andrew Viduka (1997)
Marc S. Walton (1998)
Paul Watson (1988)
Leslie Weber (2002)
Christopher White (1996)
Lisa Young (1996)

INSTITUTIONS REPRESENTED

Barnard College
Baylor University
Boston University
Bowdoin College
Brandeis University
Brown University
Bryn Mawr College
Bucknell University

Calgary University*
Cambridge University*
Carleton College
College of New Jersey
College of St. Benedict
College of William and Mary
College of Wooster
Columbia University
Concordia University*
Connecticut College
Cornell University

Dartmouth College
Duke University

Eastern Michigan University
Eckerd College
Emory University

Florida State University

George Mason University
George Washington University
Grinnell College

Hampden-Sydney College
Harvard University
Haverford College
Hillsdale College
Hollins University
Hunter College

Indiana University

Loyola Marymount University

McMaster University*
Michigan State University
Middlebury College

Newcastle University*
New York University
North Carolina State University

Oberlin College
Ohio State University
Ohio Wesleyan University
Oklahoma State University
Oxford University*

Pennsylvania State University
Pomona College
Princeton University

Randolph-Macon College
Rhodes College
Rice University

Smith College
Stanford University
SUNY Buffalo

Trinity College
Tufts University
Tulane University

University of Alberta*
University of Amsterdam*
University of Arizona
University of Arkansas
University of Athens*
University of British Columbia*
University of California, Berkeley
University of California, Los Angeles
University of Chicago
University of Cincinnati
University of Georgia
University of Illinois
University of Kansas
University of Maryland

Univeristy of Maryland,
    Baltimore County
University of Michigan
University of Minnesota
University of Mississippi
University of Missouri
University of Montana
University of Nebraska
University of North Carolina
University of Northern Illinois
University of Oregon
University of Ottawa*
University of Pennsylvania
University of South Florida
University of Sydney*
University of Tennessee
University of Texas
University of Thessaloniki*
University of Toronto*
University of Uppsala*
University of Vermont .
University of Washington
University of Waterloo*
University of Vienna*
University of Virginia

Vanderbilt University
Vassar College

Wabash College
Washington University
Wayne State University
Wellesley College
Wesleyan University
Wheaton College
Wilfrid Laurier University*
Willamette University

Yale University

*Canadian or European university

267. Agora staff and student volunteers, 2005. Front row: (left to right) Jeremy Ott, James Artz, Elizabeth Cantile, Jessica Gingras, Ricardo Apostol, Brooke Masek, Aaron Palmore, Katherine Harrington, Elizabeth Zegos, Brent Bonds. Second row: Michael Decker, Tallulah Knopp, Minnie McMahon, Annmarie Bobak, Johanna Hobratschk, Meghan Gandy, Jennifer Poppel, Bonnie Wright, Jessica Paga, Gabriella Lini, Kirk Norman, Alex Walthall, Megan Thomsen, Amber DeLuca. Third row: Bruce Hartzler, Mathew Baumann, Matt McCallum, Sigrid Eliassen, Joanna Malandrenias, Daniel Sahlen, Richard Grossmann, Ashley Bones, Kristen Bellamy, Brittany Hayden, Christopher Young, Amanda Reiterman. Back row: Amandina Anastassiades, Kim Cullen Cobb, Clare Pickersgill, Claudia Chemello, Marcie Handler, Kevin Daly, Laura Gawlinski, John Camp, Michael Laughy, Anne McCabe, Rikke Berg, Fred Ley, Maria Stamatatou, Richard Anderson, Giorgos Dervos, Craig Mauzy. Missing: Victoria Brown, Sylvie Dumont, Patricia Felch, Jan Jordan, Pia Kvarnström, Irini Marathaki, Angelique Sideris, Melina Smirniou, Vassilis Spanos.